Pacific Asia in the 1990s

The Royal Institute of International Affairs is an independent body which promotes the rigorous study of international questions and does not express opinions of its own. The opinions expressed in this publication are the responsibility of the authors.

Pacific Asia in the 1990s

Masahide Shibusawa,
Zakaria Haji Ahmad and
Brian Bridges

ROUTLEDGE
London and New York
for
**THE ROYAL INSTITUTE OF
INTERNATIONAL AFFAIRS**

First published 1992
by Routledge
11 New Fetter Lane, London EC4P 4EE

Simultaneously published in the USA and Canada
by Routledge
29 West 35th Street, New York, NY 10001

Reprinted 1993

© 1992 Royal Institute of International Affairs
Typeset in Baskerville by
Input Typesetting Ltd, London
Printed in Great Britain by
Antony Rowe Ltd, Chippenham, Wiltshire

British Library Cataloguing in Publication Data
Shibusawa, Masahide
   Pacific Asia in the 1990s.
   1. East Asia. Foreign relations
   I. Title II. Ahmad, Zakaria Haji *1947–* III. Bridges, Brian
   327.0951

ISBN 0–415–02173–1

Library of Congress Cataloging in Publication Data
Shibusawa, Masahide, 1925–
   Pacific Asia in the 1990s / Masahide Shibusawa, Zakaria Haji
   Ahmad, and Brian Bridges.
      p. cm
   Published for the Royal Institute of International Affairs.
   Includes bibliographical references and index.
   ISBN 0–415–02173–1
   1. Japan—Economic conditions—1989– 2. Economic forecasting—
Japan. 3. East Asia—Economic conditions. 4. Economic
forecasting—East Asia. 5. Asia, Southeastern—Economic conditions.
6. Economic forecasting—Asia, Southeastern. I. Zakaria bin Haji
Ahmad. 1947– . II. Bridges, Brian, 1948– . III. Royal
Institute of International Affairs. IV. Title
HC462.95.S55   1992
330.95′001′12—dc20   91–12916
                                                              CIP

Contents

Preface

This volume reflects the long-standing interest of the Royal Institute of International Affairs in the Pacific Asian region. Masahide Shibusawa, having written one book for the Institute in 1984 (*Japan and the Asian Pacific Region: Profile of Change*, RIIA/Croom Helm), felt that it was important to continue to follow developments in this part of the world – an area so notably still in a state of flux. By combining with two co-authors, he has endeavoured to encourage complementary inputs from the varying perspectives of a Northeast Asian, a Southeast Asian and someone from outside the region. The three authors readily agreed to a certain amount of burden-sharing, each taking primary responsibility for the first draft of specific chapters, which were then revised and rewritten in the light of co-authors' and others' comments. The chapters can stand on their own, but they also feed into and reflect on the predominant themes of the book.

We toyed with various names for the region under study. In settling on 'Pacific Asia', we have taken the term to refer primarily to the countries which border the western rim of the Pacific Ocean: namely Japan, North and South Korea, China, Taiwan and Hong Kong, through to the three Indochinese states of Vietnam, Laos and Cambodia and the six states of ASEAN (the Association of Southeast Asian Nations), namely Brunei, Indonesia, Malaysia, the Philippines, Singapore and Thailand. The activities of the two superpowers, the Soviet Union and the United States, and other countries either close to or involved in the region, are examined as and when their actions touch on the themes of the study.

* * *

Members of staff at Chatham House played crucial roles in putting the book together. Special appreciation goes to Pauline Wickham, who took time off to travel to Japan to help combine three very different approaches and writing styles. With outstanding skill and judgment, she was able to organize various manuscripts into a coherent whole. Kate Grosser, then a Research Associate on the International Economics Programme, helped to provide much of the economic data. For grappling with a variety of disks and formats, Shyama Iyer deserves our gratitude, and thanks go too to Hannah Doe, Gabrielle Galligan, Monica Shen, Lucy McDermot, Kathy Oswald and Lau Beng Thye, all of whom have lent a hand. Peter Ferdinand, Head of the Asia-Pacific Programme at Chatham House, has been a patient and sympathetic guide.

We are particularly grateful to the following institutions for their generous financial support, without which this project would not have been possible: Royal International Insurance, the GB–Sasakawa Foundation, the Kearny Foundation (Hong Kong) and the East–West Seminar (Tokyo).

The geographical separation of the work-places of the three authors has served as both a reason and an excuse for meetings around the world, in London, Kuala Lumpur, Tokyo and Anchorage, as the research and writing progressed. Drafts of various chapters have been discussed at study groups and conferences in London (organized by the Royal Institute of International Affairs) and in Kuala Lumpur (under the auspices of the Malaysian International Affairs Forum); we wish to thank those who participated for their comments and suggestions. We would also like to express thanks to Ahn Byung-joon, Douglas Barry, Paul Chan, Paul Johnson, DeAnne Julius, R. A. Longmire, Shiro Saito, Gerald Segal, Sully Taylor and R. Vaitheswaran, all of whom have commented in detail on parts of the book; any mistakes and misrepresentations, however, are our responsibility.

Last, but not least, we wish to thank our wives for their forbearance and encouragement over such a long period.

Masahide Shibusawa
Zakaria Haji Ahmad
Brian Bridges

Introduction

The 1980s was a period of great change for Pacific Asia. China surprised the world by beginning the decade with an ambitious programme of modernization, which it had to abandon in tragic circumstance at its end. For the non-socialist countries, however, it turned out to be another decade of robust growth, when they demonstrated their remarkable economic resilience by overcoming the global recession of the mid-1980s and bouncing back to high growth. For all the reservations that Asia-watchers may have, the region enters the 1990s confident and brimming with optimism.

Japanese economists like to refer to the phenomenon of East Asian growth as the 'flying-geese pattern', with Japan at the head, followed by the four high-flying newly industrializing economies (NIEs) – South Korea, Taiwan, Hong Kong and Singapore – and then the ASEAN countries, in a regular formation, with shifting comparative advantage as the countries advance in technological sophistication. The flying-geese pattern is said to differ from the more traditional vertical international division of labour, in that there is competition as well as complementarity, which makes it more dynamic.

But Pacific Asia's dynamism will not exonerate the countries of the region from paying the costs of success or the price of maturity. The rapidly changing structure of the world economy will surely present a new set of problems and challenges. The socio-political systems that fostered economic growth so effectively in the past will need to make major adjustments to cope with the new environment. The emerging new pattern of East–West relations will call for a different regional security structure. In the chapters that follow, we examine these and other aspects of Pacific Asia's development, and attempt to assess how the region will respond to the challenges of the 1990s and beyond.

The treatment is thematic, rather than comprehensive, focusing on two themes: economic development, and regional and global interdependence. Economic development in the region, the book's central theme, is seen as having acquired its specifically Pacific Asian characteristics as a result of certain conditions that have tended to recur in the political environment of the countries concerned. Pacific Asia's increasingly intricate patterns of economic and political interdependence – both at the regional and, still more, at the global level – run through the book as a subsidiary theme, pointing to some of the challenges and opportunities that lie ahead as the Pacific Asian economies attain maturity. The first three chapters provide the context for the more detailed discussion of the later chapters. They seek to identify those factors – whether in the economic or in the security environment – that have made the region important and successful. The later chapters, building on these themes, then look at the specific ways in which individual countries, or groups of countries, have handled the issues raised in the first three chapters.

Chapter 1 provides an overview of the region's economy, analyses some of the strategies underlying the sustained impressive performance of Pacific Asia's non-socialist economies, and considers whether these strategies will be equally effective in the changing conditions of the 1990s. It looks in particular at the shifting patterns of interaction with the outside world, by means of trade, investment and aid, and above all by the multinationalization of Asian companies – a process that ignores national and political divisions.

Chapter 2 looks at the regional security environment, in which national security issues relate as much to domestic developments as to external aggression. It argues, furthermore, that external factors in the security environment, such as the US 'security umbrella', have been particularly favourable to the region's economic growth, and it speculates on a post-cold-war future that is marked by a reduced US military presence.

Chapter 3 experiments with building a model that might throw some light on Pacific Asian economic dynamism. It seeks to identify the correlation between economic growth and political factors (domestic and external), in an effort to determine whether any particular combination of conditions can help to explain the success of the Pacific Asian developmental state.

We then move on to the more detailed discussion of groups of countries and individual countries. Chapters 4 and 5 both deal with the former category. Chapter 4 considers the four NIEs, the region's high-flyers and the epitome of its economic dynamism. It is primarily these countries that are feeling the social and political strains that accompany economic maturity.

Chapter 5 looks at various regional groupings in Southeast Asia, focusing on the ASEAN member-states, whose apparent ability to act unilaterally and multilaterally at one and the same time provides a unique example of regional collaboration. The ASEAN countries have developed their own brand of Pacific Asian pragmatism, which enables them to take from the regional and extra-regional environment those elements that suit their national purposes.

Chapter 6 describes the attempt of the Chinese leadership, under Deng Xiaoping, to tap into the region's economic dynamism, and analyses some of the difficulties experienced by China, as well as by North Korea and Vietnam, in trying to blend two systems. It also discusses the significance of the repression of the pro-democracy movement in China in mid-1989, which is presented as symbolizing a turning-point in Pacific Asian affairs.

Chapter 7 considers the special position of Japan as an economic locomotive in the region, and looks for reasons in the national psyche that make it unable, or unwilling, to assume a leadership role. It suggests that, instead, Japan might take on the task of facilitator, acting in tandem with the United States in a supportive capacity.

Chapter 8 reviews the issues discussed, and offers a concluding glimpse into the near future.

Chapter 1

The region's economy
Patterns of prosperity

The 1980s proved to be a boom decade for the Pacific Asian economies. Their performance was remarkable by any standards – for developing or developed countries alike. According to World Bank figures for 1980–9, Pacific Asia's developing countries averaged real GDP growth rates of 8.4 per cent, as against 1.6 per cent for Latin America, 2.9 per cent for the Middle East and North Africa, and 3.0 per cent for the industrial countries. Moreover, they achieved these high average rates in spite of setbacks resulting from the mid-decade global recession (both Singapore and the Philippines recorded negative growth during this period on occasion) – once again demonstrating the region's resilience and extraordinary economic thrust.

This chapter considers some of the trends underlying the sustained impressive performance and shifting comparative advantage – the 'flying-geese pattern' – of the major Pacific Asian economies. It examines the individual growth patterns of the various parts of the region during the 1980s; looks at their links with each other and with the major non-regional economies through flows of trade, investment and aid; and, in the final section, summarizes how these flows are changing and what such changes may imply for the degree of interdependence both within the region and between the region and the rest of the global economy.

The chapter focuses on the region's non-socialist economies: those of Japan, the four NIEs (Hong Kong, Singapore, South Korea and Taiwan) and the ASEAN group, minus Singapore (which is clearly better treated as an NIE). The important new role of China, the only socialist country to be included, is addressed whenever the restructuring of the region is being considered.

REGIONAL GROWTH PATTERNS

Part of the interest of Pacific Asia's flying-geese pattern lies in the fact that these geese are not of the same size or breed, nor are they flying at the same speed. Thus the resource-rich ASEAN countries contrast with the resource-poor NIEs and Japan; per capita income levels – see Table 1 – range from over $21,000 per year in Japan (one of the highest in the world) to around $300 per year in China (one of the lowest); and export levels show equally great variations – from the extremes of the city-states of Singapore and Hong Kong, whose annual exports exceed their total GNP, to China and Japan, where, surprisingly, exports are below 15 per cent of GNP.

Table 1 Economic indicators of the region

	Population (1988, mn)	GDP (1988 $ bn)	GNP (per capita 1988)	GDP growth rate (1980–8)	Growth of exports (1980–8)
Japan	123	2,844	21,020	3.9	5.3
Singapore	3	24	9,070	5.7	7.3
Hong Kong	6	45	9,220	7.3	12.3
South Korea	42	171	3,600	9.9	14.7
Taiwan	20	122	6,177	6.7	13.0
Malaysia	17	35	1,940	4.6	9.4
Thailand	55	58	1,000	6.0	11.3
Philippines	60	39	630	0.1	0.4
Indonesia	175	83	440	5.1	2.9
China	1,088	372	330	10.3	11.9

Source: World Bank, *World Development Report, 1990* (Oxford: Oxford University Press, 1990); Executive Yuan, *Statistical Yearbook of the Republic of China, 1989* (Taipei, 1989).

Growth rates, too, have differed widely. Taking the whole of the economic cycle 1980–8, China recorded the highest average annual growth rate for the region at just over 10 per cent. The NIEs were the strongest performers in the 1986–8 period, but by the very end of the decade they had been overtaken by two ASEAN countries, Malaysia and, above all, Thailand. Performance in the ASEAN countries varied greatly during the decade. Several were hit by commodity price declines in the first half of the 1980s, but they recovered to good rates of growth by the end of the decade, led, as noted, by Thailand and Malaysia. Indonesia was hit badly by the fall in oil prices, but managed an average growth rate of 5 per cent in the years 1986–9. The mid-1990 global rises in the price of oil are likely to benefit the ASEAN oil producers – Malaysia, Indonesia and Brunei – but to handicap the importers, Thailand and the Philippines. The Philippines had already suffered in the first half of the 1980s as political upheaval, brought on in part by economic corruption and mismanagement, resulted in an absolute fall in GNP by more than 10 per cent during 1984–5. The economy began slowly to recover, thanks to a drastic stabilization programme supported by financial resources from the IMF and the World Bank, until it was hit again in 1990 by natural disasters, political uncertainties and rising oil prices.

As for external debt, although the Pacific Asian countries have not developed the huge debts associated with Latin America, several of them did experience considerable increases in outstanding debt and debt-service ratios during the 1980s (see Table 2). For some, such as Thailand and Malaysia, the structural adjustment now being undertaken is preventing debt-servicing from becoming a major problem; similarly, South Korea, whose external debt peaked at $47 billion in 1985, managed to cut this right back during the second half of the 1980s. But for Indonesia and the Philippines, where export earnings stagnated and import substitution ruled for too long, external debt does give rise to serious concern. The Philippines, in fact, is listed among the world's 17

Table 2 Pacific Asian countries with largest external debt

	1980		1987	
	Debt	Debt service ratio	Debt	Debt service ratio
South Korea	18,236	12.3	30,644	21.9
Indonesia	18,113	7.9	45,389	27.9
Malaysia	5,198	2.5	21,675	14.3
Philippines	8,981	7.1	23,837	22.7
Thailand	5,773	5.0	17,131	13.6
China	4,504	4.6	23,659	7.1

Source: World Bank, *World Debt Tables, 1988–9* (Washington, 1988). Total long-term debt disbursed and outstanding in US $ million; total debt service as a percentage of exports of goods and services.

most highly indebted countries (the countries that are the focus of US Treasury Secretary Nicholas Brady's multilateral debt-reduction plan announced in 1989) – the only Pacific Asian country to be so listed.

In the NIEs, output growth during the 1980s was in the 5–8 per cent range, which is lower than it was in earlier decades, largely as a result of the global recession of the early 1980s, but still high by world standards. During this time of recession the deceleration of growth in Taiwan and South Korea was exacerbated by unfavourable domestic developments. Hong Kong and Singapore by contrast, were able to sustain output growth in the early 1980s by expanding their service sectors – particularly construction in the case of Singapore. But both of these two small economies faced renewed problems in 1985: in Singapore, wage increases and the completion of major housing and infrastructure projects reduced competitiveness; in Hong Kong, uncertainty about the territory's future political status weakened domestic demand and investment. By 1986, however, growth had resumed in all of the NIEs, and this continued strongly into 1987 and 1988; only in 1989 did these economies begin again to slow down. The oil-price rises in mid-1990 are likely to reinforce this slowing of growth among the NIEs, dependent, as they are, on importing their oil.

Japan's growth during the period 1980–9 averaged 4.2 per cent, low by earlier standards but higher than the OECD average of 2.8 per cent. As OECD growth as a whole accelerated in 1987, Japan maintained its leading position by growing at 5.4 per cent, which was also the highest growth it had recorded for fifteen years; and in 1988 and 1989 it continued to record growth rates of around 5 per cent. By regional standards, however, Japan has matured into an affluent but less dynamic economy. Nevertheless, it continues to dominate – by virtue of its sheer size. As shown in Table 1, the combined GNP of the NIEs and ASEAN is still less than one-third that of Japan. Even if China's GNP of around $370 billion were added, the total would be less than half of Japan's GNP.

TRADE PATTERNS
The global context

The central element of development strategy, for many countries of the region, has been export-led growth (although often preceded by years of import substitution and industrialization in earlier decades). By 1989 Japan's share of total world exports was 9.4 per cent, compared with the United States at 12.5 per cent, while the four NIEs together took 8.5 per cent, and ASEAN 2.6 per cent. In terms of exports of manufactured goods, the NIEs make up a more important share of world exports. In 1987 these four countries accounted for 11 per cent of world manufactured exports, and for 60 per cent of manufactured exports by all developing countries.

Throughout the 1970s and 1980s, Japan and the NIEs were high-volume exporters to the United States and the EC. The NIEs have helped to shape a triangular relationship in which they have contributed to the increase in both the US deficit and the Japanese surplus. Yet since the mid-1980s the structure of this relationship has been gradually changing. Not only has domestic demand – first in Japan and then in the more closed of the NIE economies – been stimulated, but the need for the United States to reduce its trade and fiscal deficits has raised concern about the continued openness of the US economy. The progressive restructuring of trade relations in the region which is now taking place is, therefore, part of a broader restructuring process occurring in the world economy.

Trade patterns in the region have to be seen as part of a triangular relationship because Japan and the United States are important trading partners for all the Pacific Asian developing countries. Since the late 1960s Japan has functioned as an efficient base for supplying capital goods to its developing neighbours. Its own rapid industrial development created an enormous demand for raw materials and primary products from Southeast Asia, while its imports of manufactured goods from both the NIEs and ASEAN remained low. It was the United States, and to a lesser extent the EC, which became the large importers of developing Pacific Asia's manufactured goods.

Before turning to the restructuring that began to take place in the second half of the 1980s, we must first look at the major changes in exchange rates that have resulted from – and will affect the future development of – the global imbalances between the East Asia region and the US and EC.

Exchange rates

The massive appreciation of the US dollar, against both the yen and the European currencies, during the first half of the 1980s undoubtedly contributed to the strong growth of Pacific Asian exports during that period. By 1985 it was clear that the dollar had reached unsustainable heights and had led to a widening of the US trade deficit that was beginning to threaten global financial stability. The turnaround in the yen/dollar rate began in February 1985 and was accelerated by the Plaza Agreement of September 1985, when the five key-currency countries known as the Group of Five, or G-5 (France, West Germany, Japan, the United Kingdom and the United States), made a public commitment to work together to manage a dollar depreciation. This process continued until February 1987, when, in the Louvre Accord, the G-5 declared that the dollar had fallen far enough and that the central banks would henceforth work together to stabilize exchange rates roughly at their current levels. Since then, the process of coordinated exchange-rate management has had its ups and downs, but, relative to the Pacific Asian currencies, there has not been a recurrence of the major fluctuations in yen and dollar rates that marked the 1985–7 period (see Table 3).

All of the Asian currencies depreciated strongly against the yen during those years. The currencies of Korea, Hong Kong and Malaysia basically floated down with the dollar, thereby maintaining the competitiveness of their exports to the United States as the dollar fell. Singapore, Taiwan and Thailand allowed their currencies to appreciate slightly (5–11 per cent) against the dollar. The three poorest countries of the region – China, Indonesia and the Philippines – all registered significant currency depreciation against both the dollar and the yen. Between 1987 and mid-1990, however, exchange-rate fluctuations in the region were less dramatic, the Korean won's appreciation against the dollar (up by 16 per cent from October 1987 to October 1989) being the most notable.

The most crucial exchange rate for the region remains, of course, the yen/dollar one. After the massive appreciation of the yen at the time of the Plaza Agreement (230 yen to the dollar), the rate settled down at 120 yen to the dollar, and remained relatively stable until early 1989. The yen then began to weaken (reaching

Table 3 Regional exchange rates (percentage change between February 1985 and February 1987)

	Against the yen	Against the dollar
Japanese yen	—	+41.0
Chinese yuan	−55.0	−32.0
Indonesia rupiah	−61.0	−51.0
Malaysian dollar	−40.0	+0.4
Philippine peso	−47.0	−12.0
Thai baht	−36.0	+7.0
Hong Kong dollar	−41.0	+0.2
Korean won	−42.0	−2.0
Singapore dollar	−38.0	+5.0
Taiwan dollar	+34.0	+11.0

Source: IMF, *International Financial Statistics*, various years/National statistics for Hong Kong and Taiwan. A negative sign denotes a depreciation against the reference currency.

160 yen in April 1990), but the outbreak of tension in the Middle East in August 1990 depressed the dollar and allowed it to strengthen again. The NIEs actually benefited significantly from the 1987–8 appreciation of the yen, because although the costs of their imports from Japan rose, they were able to cut a swathe out of the Japanese share of the US market (because their currencies were either pegged to the dollar or appreciated only mildly). Since then, the situation has become more complex, with the United States turning its attention to Asian currencies other than the yen.

The structure of Japanese trade

The two oil shocks of the 1970s altered the whole structure of Japanese industry. Huge efforts were made to conserve energy and raw materials, and the shift away from heavy and capital goods industries and towards high-technology and high value-added industries was accelerated. As Chapter 7 shows, the Japanese government turned the crisis to advantage, and used the oil shocks to dramatize the need for fundamental industrial restructuring – a reorganization that was in any case necessary as the transformation to an advanced, high-wage and high-skilled economy neared completion.[1] The sense of urgency engendered by the oil shocks enabled Japan to compress the adaptation period of its economy, and to achieve a rapid shift in comparative advantage which laid the foundation for the remarkable expansion of its exports in the early 1980s, when the world economy resumed growth.

This shift in comparative advantage is shown in the commodity composition of Japan's trade. According to data collected by the Keizai Koho Centre, textiles, ships, and iron and steel products, which together represented 29 per cent of Japanese exports in 1977, accounted for only 10 per cent in 1988. Televisions and radios declined from around 6 per cent of exports to under 2 per cent over the same period. Automobiles rose steadily throughout the 1980s until their share of export value peaked at 20 per cent in 1986; the new growth areas in the mid-1980s were video cassette recorders (VCRs) and scientific and optical equipment. On the import side, foodstuffs have remained significant, but their share of total imports has been declining since 1980. After massive increases in crude and partly refined oil imports in the 1970s, the share of this import also declined in the 1980s. Owing partly to declines in oil prices and the rise in the yen, from 1983 to 1987 the dollar value of imported oil declined by a half. Over the same period, machinery and equipment imports nearly doubled, reaching 13 per cent of total imports. Overall, the share of manufactured goods in Japanese imports rose from 24 per cent in 1983 to 49 per cent in 1987.[2]

In order to promote further structural change, the 1986 Maekawa Report, commissioned from an *ad-hoc* committee of experts by Prime Minister Nakasone, recommended that Japan should transform its economy by reducing its export orientation and stimulating imports and domestic demand. Although the report was meant as a vision for the 1990s rather than for the 1980s, some of its policy recommendations have already been implemented. A fiscal stimulus package was enacted in 1987 which, coupled with the effects of the appreciation of the yen, gave a strong boost to domestic demand, while in 1988–9 the Japanese economy clearly benefited from the threefold advantage of a strong yen, low interest rates and soft oil prices.

On the external side, the phenomenon of *endaka* (high yen) that has been operating since the Plaza Agreement has had a disappointingly small effect. The US–Japan trade balance, in particular, has shown little exchange-rate elasticity, and Japanese companies have cut margins rather than reducing market share. Japan's large trade surpluses are, in point of fact, a relatively recent phenomenon. After the oil-price-induced trade deficits of

1979–80, the Japanese trade balance swung into a surplus that grew steadily throughout the 1980s, reaching a peak of US $80 billion in 1987. It has since declined, down to $77 billion in 1988 and $65 billion in 1989. Japan's surplus is spread across most regions, including the United States, the EC and the rest of East Asia. The surplus with the United States grew during the 1980s to a peak of $53 billion in 1987, before declining to $46 billion in 1989. The surplus with the EC levelled off at about $10 billion in the early 1980s, but then rose to $17 billion in 1986 and $23 billion in 1988, before declining in 1989 to $19 billion. Throughout the 1980s, Japan has run trade surpluses with the four NIEs (growing from $14 billion in 1984 to $25 billion in 1989); it has also run a surplus with Thailand, but has been in deficit with the other four ASEAN countries (except with the Philippines in 1982–3 and 1989). However, as energy prices declined, so did the deficits with Indonesia and Brunei. As a result, Japan's overall trade surplus with the eight major East Asian economies grew from $1.2 billion in 1980 to $20.4 billion in 1989.

The size and nature of these surpluses have been a constant source of tension between Japan and its trading partners, especially the United States and the EC – a theme that Chapter 7 develops. Whereas in the late 1960s and 1970s the Japan–US conflicts were basically trade-related, in the 1980s they broadened to policy problems that were thought to affect trade flows, such as exchange-rate realignment, financial deregulation, and performance and safety standards procedures. The US–Japanese Structural Impediments Initiative (SII) talks in 1989–90 typified the widening range of US concern.

The problems of US–Japanese trade and broader economic relations have had an important impact on the rest of the East Asian region. On the one hand, tensions in the US–Japan relationship have overflowed into US trade relations with the NIEs, which have also built up trade surpluses with the United States. On the other hand, Japanese concessions to the United States over market-opening measures, domestic demand stimulation and yen appreciation have benefited East Asian countries too.

Certain new trends in the intra-regional trade patterns are beginning to emerge. One of the most important is that the manufactured goods of the East Asian NIEs, particularly consumer electronics, are starting to make inroads into the Japanese market. It is the NIEs, rather than the United States, which have gained the most from the yen appreciation. During the first half of the 1980s there was single-digit growth of exports from the NIEs to Japan; but following the 1985–7 appreciation of the yen, such exports accelerated, rising from $11 billion in 1985 to $25 billion in 1988. In 1987 alone the total dollar value of Japan's imports from the NIEs rose by 50 per cent over the preceding year, although by 1989 the import growth rate had dropped to 9 per cent. Moreover, the composition of imports has also been changing – from labour-intensive finished goods to technology-intensive parts and more sophisticated consumer and even capital goods. The proportion of manufactured goods in Japanese imports from the NIEs increased from 58 per cent in 1980 to 66 per cent in 1987.

A large part of this trend is the result of increased Japanese foreign direct investment (FDI) in the NIEs, as discussed in the next section of this chapter. In a survey conducted in 1988 by the Ministry of International Trade and Industry (MITI), nearly half of the 176 large Japanese manufacturing firms investigated were importing semi-finished and finished parts from their overseas plants, from partners in foreign countries with original equipment manufacturing (OEM) contracts, and from joint ventures overseas.[3]

Clearly, the impact of Japan's restructuring has been different for raw-material-based economies of ASEAN. The proportion of raw materials and fuel per unit of production has been declining in Japan since the 1970s, as it has in many other industrialized countries. The raw material producers of ASEAN, therefore, saw their exports to Japan fall from $24 billion in 1980 to $19 billion in 1988, before they revived in 1989 to $22 billion. The mid-1990 oil-price rises will benefit the ASEAN oil exporters; but, if the net effect of that price rise is to make Japan even more concerned about energy conservation, then ASEAN may have less to gain from trade links with Japan than do the NIEs of the region. ASEAN trade growth, therefore, will depend increasingly on Japanese and NIE FDI and other investments which can contribute to upgrading the industrial base of the ASEAN countries and diversifying their exports – including to the NIEs.

Of course, the picture becomes more complex when individual sectors and products are examined. Although, overall, raw material imports from Pacific Asia have become less important for Japan, it still depends on the region for its main supplies of petroleum products (Singapore) and rubber (Thailand, Malaysia and Indonesia together supplied 98 per cent of Japan's needs in 1988); and it is heavily dependent as regards wood (Malaysia), crude oil (Indonesia), copper (Philippines), sugar (Thailand) and textile materials (China). Different countries in the region act as its most important markets for textiles, textile machinery, plastic materials, electronic components, and watches and clocks.

How have these important structural changes affected interdependence between Japan and the rest of the region? From Japan's point of view, the rest of the region has become a more important source of imports and a less important export market. As shown in Table 4, however, this overall pattern conceals a shift that has taken place within the region. There has been a relative decline in the importance of Japan's trade with ASEAN over the 1980–9 period and a significant increase in the importance of its trade with the NIEs. Since 1988 Japan's trade with the four NIEs has been of roughly the same size as that with the twelve countries of the EC. In terms of relative trade importance, however, Japanese interdependence with the US market is the area showing the greatest increase during the 1980s, and is still predominant, even though it has declined from its 1987–8 peak.

Table 4 Japan's regional trade flows (percentage of trade value)

	Japanese exports		Japanese imports	
	1980	*1989*	*1980*	*1989*
Four NIEs	15	19	5	13
Five ASEAN	14	6	16	11
China	4	3	3	5
Regional total	33	28	24	29
United States	24	34	17	23
EC	14	18	6	13

Source: IMF, *Direction of Trade Statistics*, various years.

The NIEs' trade patterns

For all four NIEs, as for Japan, the most striking feature of the 1980s was the growth of exports to the United States (see Table 5). There is evidence, however, that this export dependency on the US economy peaked in 1985–6. Certainly by 1987, three of the four NIEs (Singapore followed in 1988) had managed to reduce the share of their exports going to the United States. Exports to Japan remained steady as a share of total exports, but with a slight rise in 1987–9; imports from Japan, after slowly increasing as a share of total imports for all the NIEs except Hong Kong, had fallen back by the end of the decade. China has emerged as a more important trading partner for all the NIEs and, as a result of conscious efforts to diversify import sources, the EC has also grown in importance.

Table 5 Trade patterns of the NIEs (percentage of trade value for the four economies combined)

	NIE imports		NIE exports	
	1980	*1989*	*1980*	*1989*
Other NIEs	7	11	9	11
Five ASEAN (excluding Singapore)	8	7	10	7
China	6	11	2	8
Japan	24	24	10	13
Regional total	45	53	31	39
United States	18	18	25	30
EC	8	13	14	14

Sources: IMF, *Direction of Trade Statistics*, various years; Ministry of Economic Affairs, *Foreign Trade Development of the Republic of China, 1990* (Taipei, 1990). Intra-NIE and trade with China shares may be slightly distorted through absence of official figures on Taiwanese and Korean trade with China.

Trade flows within the rest of the region vary considerably among the four NIEs. For Hong Kong, the most striking feature has been the growth in trade with China, especially in the re-export sector, where Hong Kong has become an important inter-mediary for trade between China and both Taiwan and South Korea. As a share of Hong Kong's total exports, trade with China increased from 6 per cent in 1980 to 29 per cent in 1988, before falling to 26 per cent in 1989. The share of Hong Kong's trade with the ASEAN countries has decreased during the 1980s.

For South Korea, the most important regional export market is Hong Kong, in part en route to China, while the ASEAN-5 remain important on the import side, especially raw materials from

Indonesia and Malaysia. For Singapore, trade in the region has been growing with both China and Thailand, but remains highest with Malaysia. For Taiwan, the most important aspects of regional trade have been imports from the NIEs and growing trade with China, especially exports, although much of this is still via Hong Kong (Taiwan–China trade, overall, grew from an estimated $1.5 billion in 1987 to $3.5 billion in 1989).

Significantly, exports from the NIEs to each other have grown in absolute terms during the 1980s, but not until 1988 was there any increase in relative terms. NIE trade with the ASEAN countries has actually declined in relative terms over this decade. Only in 1987 did the NIEs' imports from inside the region first exceed those from outside it; however, their exports to outside the region are still far more important than intra-regional exporting. Thus, for the NIEs, the decade of the 1980s brought an increase in regional economic integration, but it also saw a continued heavy involvement in global trading activities.

ASEAN's trading patterns

ASEAN trade is more concentrated within the region than is that of the NIEs, but, as shown in Table 6, regional trade has actually decreased slightly during the 1980s as a percentage of total ASEAN trade. The same is true as regards Japan: it continues to be an important trading partner for all members of ASEAN, but for most of them its relative importance has been decreasing. Indeed, in the 1980–9 period, the dependency of the five ASEAN raw material producers on Japan declined most clearly in exports, and dependency on Japanese imports, after some decline in the mid-1980s, had by 1989 merely returned to the levels prevailing at the beginning of the decade. Over the 1980–9 period as a whole, trade relations with the United States and the EC have not really intensified either.

For the five ASEAN members excluding Singapore (which was discussed in the section above), the growth in trade with the NIEs – by contrast with the relative decline in importance of trade with Japan – was the most significant feature of the 1980s. For Thailand, trade within the region is primarily with Singapore and then with the other NIEs, but China has become an increasingly important partner since the mid-1980s. For Malaysia, Singapore is almost as important a partner as Japan, but the other NIEs are now more important than the rest of ASEAN. The Philippines' trade is more extensive with the NIEs than with ASEAN. For Indonesia, Singapore remains the largest trading partner after Japan. Brunei, heavily dependent on energy exports, looks to Japan to take over half of its exports, and to South Korea to take a further 15 per cent; but Singapore is the main source of its imports.

Table 6 Trade patterns of the ASEAN group (percentage of trade value for five economies combined)

	ASEAN imports		ASEAN exports	
	1980	1989	1980	1989
NIEs (incl. Singapore)	15	19	15	19
Other ASEAN (excl. Singapore)	5	5	4	4
China	3	3	1	2
Japan	24	25	37	25
Regional total	47	52	57	50
United States	17	14	17	20
EC	15	14	13	15

Source: IMF, *Direction of Trade Statistics*, various years

'Diversification' has become a buzz-word among the Pacific Asian developing countries. They seek trade diversification both in the sense of export product mix and in the sense of trading partners. Although the rhetoric has often preceded the reality – in the NIEs in particular and in the ASEAN group to a lesser extent – efforts are being made to move import sources away from Japan, and export shipments away from the US market. This has meant some increased trade with the EC, and also the beginning of regional trade with China, and even with the Soviet Union and Eastern Europe.

In summary, the trade data fail to show an increase in *regional* economic interdependence relative to that with the rest of the world during the 1980s, despite the stimulus of the rising yen and the growth of domestic demand following the restructuring of the Japanese economy. They do show an increase in *global* interdependence, and particularly in the size of trade flows with the United

States. The trade policy objectives of the NIEs and the ASEAN countries favour diversification both within and beyond the Pacific Asian region. There is some evidence that a shift has already begun, from around 1987–8, towards growing regional trade with Japan at the expense of the US share, at least as far as the NIEs are concerned. But this shift is a gradual one and is brought about primarily as a result of increased Japanese FDI into the other Pacific Asian economies pulling trade along in its wake. Interdependence based on investment will build up more slowly, but it is also likely to create a deeper and more stable pattern of regional specialization that may over time tie the developing countries of Pacific Asia more firmly to Japan. In this sense, investment flows are the most important indicator of growing regional interdependence.

INVESTMENT PATTERNS

Global FDI, since 1983, has been growing at a rate far exceeding that of world trade growth. FDI flows have been largely concentrated in the G-5 countries, but in the developing world the eight major Pacific Asian economies have been important recipients. World Bank figures show that the Pacific Asian countries, as a whole, have relied less heavily on borrowing from world capital markets than other developing countries, and FDI therefore makes up a higher proportion of total capital flows. This is especially true of Singapore and Malaysia. However, domestic investment in Pacific Asia is also relatively high. In Malaysia, for example, under the New Economic Policy (NEP), the foreign share of corporate capital fell from 62 per cent in 1971 to 34 per cent in 1983 during a quadrupling of the nominal value of investment. In Singapore, FDI increased over ten times between 1970 and 1981, but local investors still retained two-thirds of total equity.

Whereas some Pacific Asian countries, such as Hong Kong and Singapore, have for a long time welcomed foreign investment, it is only recently that others, such as South Korea, have come to re-evaluate the role that it can play in their development.[4] Compared with foreign loans, FDI is seen to offer not only a more flexible financial obligation, since there is a direct link between profit remittance and project performance, but probably also greater financial stability, since capital is tied to fixed assets. In addition, it can bring with it technology, management and marketing skills, as well as capital. (The degree to which this actually happens varies enormously – much FDI involves raising money on local capital markets – and depends on how well foreign subsidiaries and investments are integrated into the local economy.) This appreciation of the non-financial spin-offs of foreign investment accounts for the region's increased openness to FDI, which has come to be recognized as important for economic development.

Japanese FDI

Japan is the largest single investor in the Pacific Asian economies as a whole, although both the US and the EC are the single most important partners for some individual countries. As shown in Table 7, the US is the largest single investor in Taiwan, Hong Kong and the Philippines, while Western Europe is the largest investor in Singapore and Malaysia. For the eight capitalist developing countries as a whole, Japan accounts for 26 per cent of the total stock of inward investment, compared with 18 per cent from the US and 15 per cent from the European countries. The table does not include China, the only regional socialist state receiving significant FDI; according to Chinese figures for 1979–87 of contracted (not necessarily realized) FDI of $23.7 billion, approximately 65% came from Hong Kong and Macao, 12 per cent from Japan and 10 per cent from the United States.

Table 7 FDI into Pacific Asia by source (stock outstanding end–1986, US $ million)

	Japan	USA	W. Europe	Others
South Korea	2,091	161	430	1,374
Taiwan	1,384	1,855	721	732
Hong Kong	514	1,032	274	2,273
Indonesia	5,251	1,216	1,863	7,479
Malaysia	816	186	1,008	961
Philippines	484	1,671	407	530
Singapore	1,347	1,711	1,902	3,385
Thailand	1,859	1,732	1,432	4,054
Totals	13,746	9,564	8,037	20,788
Percentage of overall total	26.4	18.3	15.4	39.9

Source: Based on Trilateral Commission Report No. 35, *East Asia in Transition* (1988), p. 70

Post-war Japanese investment in the region falls into four main categories:

1 Investment for resource development, especially minerals and oil. Most of such investment went to Indonesia, with the aim of ensuring energy supplies after the 1973 oil crisis. As a result, Indonesia became, and remained until the mid-1980s, Japan's second largest investment destination after the United States.[5]
2 Import-substitution industries, e.g. consumer electronics, automobile components, intermediate goods. This type of FDI has been important in the ASEAN countries and in South Korea and Taiwan.
3 Export production in developing countries, using cheap labour and investment incentives and exploiting the preferential tariffs given by other industrialized countries to exports from the less developed countries (LDCs). Much Japanese investment in the NIEs and in Export Processing Zones of the ASEAN-4 has been in manufacturing industries for third-market exports. Nomura Research Institute statistics suggest that, in 1987, 59 per cent of the production of Japanese manufacturing subsidiaries in Pacific Asia was for the local market, 17 per cent for export back to Japan and 24 per cent for export to the rest of the world.[6]
4 Investment in the service sector. Since the early 1980s, Hong Kong and Singapore have been the main beneficiaries as Japanese banks, securities and insurance companies have expanded their operations. According to JETRO, 77 per cent of Japanese investment into Singapore in 1988 was in non-manufacturing businesses.

Japanese FDI was very low until the capital liberalization moves and the yen appreciation of 1969–71. The eight major Pacific Asian countries received around 15 per cent of total Japanese FDI in 1970. This percentage had doubled by 1975. In 1980, measured in cumulative totals, Asia had received 27.2 per cent of total Japanese FDI, virtually all of this going to the eight countries under review. However, from the beginning of the 1980s the share of Japanese FDI going to developed countries – especially the United States – rose dramatically. As a result, although the total Japanese FDI into Pacific Asia also rose significantly, the Pacific

Asian annual share fell gradually, reaching a low of 10.4 per cent in 1986.

Although the import-substitution strategy of investing in the United States and the EC has not been abandoned, the rapid appreciation of the yen from 1985 onwards, and the consequent restructuring of many Japanese industries, have involved moving production offshore. This has resulted in greatly increased investment in Pacific Asia. The prime potential beneficiaries are the NIEs, since it will help them to upgrade their own industrial structure to a higher technological base, to increase capital-intensive exports to Japan and elsewhere, and to encourage NIE firms to relocate labour-intensive production into ASEAN and China. In the case of the ASEAN countries, large public sectors and problems of export concentration have led them to embrace FDI as a means of helping the balance of payments without adding to debt problems. Competitive domestic exchange rates *vis-à-vis* the yen are crucial to this strategy, as is upgrading the technology know-how of the population.

After averaging around US $10 billion per annum for the first half of the 1980s, total Japanese FDI leapt up to $22.3 billion in FY 1986 and $33.4 billion in FY 1987. As shown in Table 8, it increased by a further 40 per cent in both FY 1988 and FY 1989 to reach $67 billion. The Pacific Asian share of this expanded FDI began to increase in 1987, when it reached 13.8 per cent, only to fall again to 10.2 per cent in FY 1988; in FY 1989 it recovered to 12 per cent. That represented an input to the Pacific Asian economy of $8.1 billion in FY 1989 alone. Japanese FDI in the NIEs tended to stagnate slightly in the first half of the 1980s, but in 1986–7 there were marked increases in the flows into South Korea and Taiwan, and in 1988–9, as labour costs there rose, into Hong Kong and Singapore. The upward trend is also clear in Japanese FDI in ASEAN since 1986; this too has been concentrated in the manufacturing sector. Thailand and Malaysia, in particular, have experienced a boom in Japanese investment, and only in the Philippines has Japanese FDI been rather stagnant since the early 1980s.

It is not just the quantity of FDI that is changing; two other new trends are discernible:

1 As a result of rising wage costs and currency appreciation in the NIEs, Japanese companies that produce key technology-intensive products have begun to diversify away from production

Table 8 Japan's FDI in Pacific Asia (totals in US $ million, for fiscal years)

	1951–87	1988	1989
NIEs 4	11,753	3,264	4,900
ASEAN 5	12,892	1,966	2,782
China	1,739	296	438
Outside region	112,950	41,518	59,420
Total	139,334	47,044	67,540

Source: Japanese Ministry of Finance figures, 1990

in the NIEs and move to the ASEAN countries. For example, in the autumn of 1988 Mitsubishi Electric decided to cut down audio equipment production at its Taiwanese affiliate company and increase investment in its Thai joint venture. In the autumn of 1989, Asics, the leading Japanese sports equipment manufacturer, decided to shift all its sports shoe production from South Korea to Indonesia. In FY 1988, therefore, Japanese FDI into South Korea decreased by about half, and increased more than threefold into Thailand.

2 Japanese companies are establishing more sophisticated factories in Pacific Asia and exporting higher-value-added products from the region. Although this is helping the trade balance of these countries with Japan, the balance-of-payments effect is compromised by the increasing volume and price, in yen, of imported components. A restructuring that involved more use of local components and skills would be a better long-term prospect. Examples of upgraded Japanese investment are Sony's new expansion of manufacturing of compact disc players in Singapore, which marked the first transfer from Japan of Sony's large-scale robotized production system for optical pick-ups, and Fujitsu's plans to build a $25 million semi-conductor plant in Malaysia.

However, Japanese FDI can be seen as having some unfavourable side-effects. For example, in Thailand, land prices, at industrial complexes especially, have been rising as a direct result of the rush of Japanese investment there. There is also some fear of the political consequences of these new flows, such as Japanese involvement in local labour disputes and a recurrence of the early 1970s perceived 'over-presence' of Japanese.

FDI by the Asian NIEs

A further new trend is beginning to emerge in regional FDI – again caused by rising wage costs and currency appreciation in the NIEs – and that is an increase from the NIEs themselves of FDI in the region. Both home- and host-country data show an increase in NIE FDI into ASEAN since the mid-1980s.[7] South Korean FDI into ASEAN amounted to over US $250 million in cumulative stock in 1988, with flows of $177 million in 1986–8 alone, triple the flows of 1981–5. From Taiwan, FDI into ASEAN is estimated to have reached a cumulative total of $86 million between 1959 and 1987, of which approximately $35 million was invested in 1984–7. Typical of the increased Taiwanese FDI is the $220 million petrochemical plant joint venture in the Philippines (that country's largest equity investment for a decade) and a $1 billion 'electronics park' planned for Malaysia.[8] Hong Kong has often been reported to be the greatest provider of FDI into the region from the four NIEs; official data are not available, but it seems that China has been the main beneficiary in the 1980s (according to Chinese data, Hong Kong and Macao invested $15.5 billion during 1979–87). Flows from Singapore into other ASEAN countries have also been growing, but not as rapidly as from the other NIEs because, in contrast with South Korea and Taiwan, there has been little appreciation of the Singapore dollar and Singapore itself went through a recession in 1985–6.

It is significant that whereas FDI from the NIEs into ASEAN has grown enormously in absolute terms, and has increased in relative importance for nearly all the recipient countries, it has declined in relative importance for the NIEs themselves, especially for Taiwan and South Korea, which have increasingly invested in the United States. For Taiwan, up to 1979 over half of outward FDI went to ASEAN, and 15 per cent went to the United States. In 1980–3 the ASEAN share fell below 30 per cent while the US share rose to 56 per cent, and in 1984–7 the ASEAN share dropped to 14 per cent while the US share rose to 76 per cent. The same pattern is seen in South Korea. Between 1968 and 1974, 82 per cent of Korean FDI went to Asia and Oceania and 10% to the

United States, while by 1987 only 34 per cent went to the former areas and 45 per cent to the United States.

Until recently, the NIEs have tended to invest in industries at the mature end of the product cycle, where operations were labour-intensive and cost was very important, the most popular industries being textiles, garments, plastics, wood-processing and labour-intensive electronics. Moreover, NIE FDI in ASEAN has been especially strong in manufacturing. Now, however, the pattern is becoming more diversified. In the period 1959–83, almost all of Taiwan's FDI in ASEAN was in manufacturing, especially in chemical products, textiles, pulp and paper, but in 1984–7 the manufacturing share shrank to 80 per cent, as construction and service-sector FDI grew. In fact there was a decline in the manufacturing share of Taiwanese FDI in all countries except Indonesia, and this was especially evident in the Philippines and Thailand, where the relative importance of the construction industry has grown enormously.

Hong Kong's FDI in ASEAN is diversified into three main sectors, services, manufacturing and agriculture. Services FDI from Hong Kong has been particularly important in Indonesia, and Thai data for 1983–6 show 50–70 per cent of Hong Kong's inward FDI going into financial institutions. Singapore's FDI in Malaysia has also had a high services content. FDI from the other NIEs into Singapore has been relatively very insignificant because of similarities of levels of development and of labour costs in these countries. Finally, it is important to note that recently China has become a favoured host for the relocation of labour-intensive production, not just from Hong Kong, but also from the other three NIEs, such as from Taiwan via Hong Kong, and increasingly via direct contacts.

The NIEs themselves have a comparative advantage in technology-intensive products, but still lack advantage in physical capital-intensive production, for which they rely on Japanese FDI. Their role as transferers of technology, however, in terms of plants, consultancy, capital, licensing, training and managerial skills is becoming increasingly evident, and the relative importance of new forms of 'unpackaged' FDI in the region is notable in these cases.

Intra-regional trade is, for the most part, a very recent phenomenon, so it is difficult to generalize about its character or likely effects on future development. Japan's investment projects in Asia are on average one-sixth of the size of its average investment project in the US and the EC. While these smaller projects are described as being more appropriate to the needs of Asian countries, there is a major question about transfer of technology from Japanese FDI. Many argue that the Japanese record in this regard has not been as good as that of US- and EC-based companies. With respect to the flows from the NIEs into ASEAN, there is evidence to suggest that there are important differences between developing-country multinationals and those from industrialized countries. Developing-country multinationals tend to establish joint ventures with local partners, whereas industrial country multinationals are more likely to establish wholly owned subsidiaries. Developing-country multinationals usually establish within their own regional sphere, and usually have smaller-scale production processes and less capital-intensive technology. They also show a greater propensity to transfer this technology than do the more sophisticated multinationals from industrialized countries.[9]

As with trade flows, the FDI patterns show an increase in the size and diversity of flows among the Pacific Asian economies, but at the same time they fail to show an overall *relative* increase in regional interdependence. A rather greater increase in FDI from Japan and the NIEs has been to countries outside the region; in particular, to the United States (by FY 1988 the US share of Japanese FDI had risen to 46 per cent).[10] However, for many of the FDI *host* countries in the region the importance of FDI from the region has grown enormously in relative terms. FDI from Japan has grown faster than any other FDI into ASEAN and into several of the NIEs. For these countries, dependence on regional sources of FDI (including technology and capital) has grown in absolute and relative terms, and this will affect regional flows in the future.

DEVELOPMENT AID PATTERNS

Just as Japan plays a crucial role for the other Pacific Asian economies as a trading partner and as a source of investment funds, so it is also a major provider of official development assistance (ODA). In 1989 Japan overtook the United States to become the world's largest aid donor to developing countries. Its announced commitments of $50 billion for the years 1988–92 are expected to double the volume of its ODA disbursements in the preceding five-year period. Unfortunately, its aid programme suffers from poor coordination (as many as 17 ministries and agencies are involved, directly or indirectly, in cooperation with developing countries) and shortages of personnel and expertise.

Traditionally, Japan's aid has been concentrated in Asia. From the 1960s through to the early 1970s, between 90 per cent and 100 per cent of total Japanese bilateral ODA went to Asian countries. In the late 1970s, aid to Middle Eastern, African and Latin American countries increased, and the share going to Asian countries has now levelled off at about 70 per cent. Around half of this, 30% of the total, goes to ASEAN countries. Since 1982 China has been the largest recipient of Japan's bilateral ODA, followed by the ASEAN four of Thailand, Indonesia, the Philippines and Malaysia. Although the diversification of Japanese ODA to other continents will be speeded up in the coming years, Japan is likely to remain Pacific Asia's main provider. According to OECD figures for 1988, Japan accounted for the following percentages of official bilateral aid: 68 per cent for the Philippines, 70 per cent for Thailand, 56 per cent for China, 66 per cent for Indonesia.

In the case of the ASEAN countries, and indeed of China, the link between ODA and investment is important. At the ASEAN summit meeting in December 1987, Japan announced a $2 billion aid package, given as loans over three years, and aimed at promoting private-sector joint ventures between Japanese and other regional companies and ASEAN companies. In August 1988 Japan announced a $6 billion loan to China, spread over five years, and an investment protection agreement through which it would fund labour-intensive projects in China in return for tax guarantees and assured access to facilities in China's booming coastal region.

Japanese aid is being used to stimulate investment in a number of ways, including official guarantees of FDI, the development of appropriate infrastructure, and the stimulation of local equity and capital markets. Japan increasingly makes yen-denominated loans for infrastructure building in export-oriented industrial parks, and encourages software cooperation, finance and technical services to help Japanese industrial investment in Southeast Asia.

The quality of Japanese aid is often questioned. Japan has made a lower percentage of 'soft' loans than other ODA donors. In 1987 the Japanese grant element made up 75.5 per cent of aid flows, as against an average of 93.2 per cent. This is explained partly by the high percentage of Japanese aid going to Asia, where loans have been made the main tool for meeting the need for capital. As long as large proportions of Japanese aid continue to go to Asia, the loan element of its ODA will probably remain high, even as it is increasing the grant element in commitments to other areas. The grant element of ODA to ASEAN, especially the Philippines, may also increase, redressing this balance slightly.

The question of loans denominated in yen gained new significance when the yen began its rapid appreciation in 1985. This issue was raised at the 1987 ASEAN summit, and Japan announced that it was in the process of working out detailed plans to help developing countries with the problem. A possible solution was indicated in 1988, when Indonesia gained a major concession from Japan, its main bilateral donor, in its bid to reduce the yen portion of its debt (about 30 per cent of the total $40 billion). Part of the new loan agreement signed in Tokyo that July was denominated in US dollars. The Japanese EXIM Bank is to lend the equivalent of $576 million (comprising two separate elements of Y60 billion and $200 million) at semi-concessionary interest rates to fund power, transport and agricultural projects run by the World Bank and the Asian Development Bank. This was the first time that the EXIM Bank had lent in foreign currency, and it set an important precedent.

Trends over the past decade show a dramatic reduction in Japan's aid to South Korea, and a drop in the shares of Malaysia, Thailand and Indonesia, as measured on both a yen and a dollar basis. By contrast, there was an increase in aid to the Philippines, which in 1987 received 11.4 per cent of total Japanese aid. Although reluctant to admit it, ever since the early 1980s the Japanese government, under US pressure, has increasingly been taking account of the 'strategic' element in the provision of aid – that is, the role that aid can play in promoting social and political stability.[11] Aid to Thailand and South Korea in the early 1980s, as well as, more recently, to the Philippines, reflect this consideration. Discussions among policy-makers of the United States, Japan and other OECD countries about the feasibility of creating some kind of new 'Marshall Plan' to assist developing countries (primarily through a recycling of the Japanese trade surplus) have tended to focus on the Philippines, through the Multinational Assistance Initiative (MAI), as the most likely East Asian recipient. The July 1989 multinational conference in Tokyo, which launched the Philippines MAI, envisaged a four-year programme of soft loans, topped up with some grants; although the United States and the EC made substantial commitments, the Japanese pledge was by far the largest. The Japanese government's aid commitments may also be taken as trying to encourage Japanese commercial investors,[12] whose concern about the medium-term political stability of the Philippines has recently left it languishing as the least popular site for Japanese FDI out of the eight major East Asian economies.

One new trend in development assistance is the beginning of aid flows from the NIEs to the region. In 1988 Taiwan established a soft-loan fund of $1.2 billion, to be disbursed to developing countries over a five-year period. This is being used to help with infrastructural projects, to assist Taiwanese companies in investing overseas, to fund technical cooperation, and to enhance trade – and in some cases diplomatic – relations, and is concentrated first and foremost on 'friendly' developing countries in Southeast Asia and Africa. It will help reduce Taiwan's massive foreign-exchange reserves, which reached $76 billion at the end of 1987, and is being managed by Taiwan's EXIM Bank. As with Japanese aid, there is a clear link between this and Taiwanese investment. In August 1987 South Korea launched its own economic development cooperation fund, which will distribute 60 billion won of currency loans, 55 billion of which will be assigned to developing countries in order to finance development projects and capital goods purchase. This is part of a plan to lend 300 billion won over the five-year period 1987–91. Having virtually ceased to receive any ODA themselves, South Korea and Taiwan are likely gradually to expand their role as donors.

EXTRA-REGIONAL PARTNERS

Extra-regional partners – the United States and the EC in particular – have almost as important a role, or potential role, as Japan in the regional matrix of trade, aid and investment. The United States has an important stake itself in Pacific Asia; the Europeans less evidently so, though it is a region that they ignore at the risk of missing major economic opportunities in the 1990s.

The United States

The foundation of the US economic relationship with Pacific Asia is merchandise trade; since 1982 that trade has exceeded its trade with the European members of the OECD. The expansion of Pacific Asian exports to the US market during the 1980s has created competitive difficulties for a number of US industries, and has contributed to the rise of protectionist tendencies. Although the causes of the huge overall US trade deficit lie predominantly in macroeconomic policies, the deficit with Japan and the Asian NIEs has taken on, for the Americans, a symbolic value, which makes it loom larger than deficits with other regions of the world.

Throughout the 1970s, despite the trade-diverting influence of the oil-price rises, the Pacific Asian share of US exports and imports remained roughly constant. Then, in the 1980s, it rose from around 20 per cent in 1980 to 25 per cent in 1988, while the region's share of US imports increased from 25 per cent in 1980 to 37 per cent in 1988. The commodity range and geographical pattern of US trade with Pacific Asia reflects the diversity of the economies in the region. The United States exports high-technology and capital-intensive manufactures to all the Pacific Asian economies, and agricultural products to resource-poor NIEs Japan. US imports are overwhelmingly manufactured goods, plus a small amount of oil (mainly from Indonesia). During the 1980s the USA's trade deficits with the four NIEs increased even more spectacularly (from a smaller base) than that with Japan – from $3.2 billion in 1980 to a huge $31.6 billion in 1987. For almost all the developing Pacific Asian countries, the share of exports going to the US increased during the first half of the 1980s (Taiwan was the most exposed in 1984, when 49 per cent of its total exports went to the United States), but during 1987–8 they were all able to start reducing their dependency on the US market.

FDI from the United States to the region parallels the motives, and often the patterns, of Japanese FDI. Japan is the most important single recipient of US FDI in the region, though accounting for only around 5 per cent of total US FDI in cumulative terms in 1989. FDI is primarily aimed at manufacturing for the Japanese domestic market, and in 1985 local sales by US-affiliated firms in Japan were only slightly below the US export total to Japan for that year. Exporting back to the United States is a less important motive, but in 1986 9 per cent of total US imports from Japan came from US affiliates there.[13] Other important recipients are Indonesia (the petroleum/gas sector), Hong Kong and Singapore. It was estimated in 1986 that about one-third of US-owned manufacturing output in the NIEs and ASEAN went to the United

States and two-fifths to respective domestic markets. About one-fifth of all US imports (including natural resources) from these countries came from US overseas affiliates.[14] US FDI to the region apart from Japan has grown both in real terms and as a percentage of total US FDI (from 4 per cent of flows in 1980 to around 6 per cent in 1989). The United States is, of course, itself a recipient of FDI from Pacific Asia. However, in the second half of the 1980s the flow of Japanese FDI into the United States was far larger than the reverse flow of US FDI into Japan (in FY 1989 Japanese FDI into the United States totalled $32.5 billion, but US FDI into Japan only $1.6 billion). Although much more limited in amount and objective, South Korea and Taiwan are also beginning to invest in the United States.

US development aid to Pacific Asia has been less than EC aid to the region throughout the 1980s, and far less than Japanese aid. The economic strength of the NIEs ensured that by the mid-1980s there was a net outflow from them back to the United States. The bulk of US aid has gone to the Philippines – a reflection of the uncertain economic and political conditions there. Annual flows to the Philippines rose from $50 million in 1980 to $351 million in 1986 (by then nearly three-quarters of all US bilateral aid to the region), before declining to $78 million in 1988. US commercial bank lending to the developing Pacific Asian countries is also extensive, estimated at $41 billion (outstanding at the end of March 1985), more than three times the US FDI.

The US government, particularly under President Reagan, toyed with the idea of establishing Free Trade Agreements (FTAs) with certain Pacific Asian countries as a means of managing economic relationships. As long ago as 1984 a proposal for a US–ASEAN FTA was floated, but owing to ASEAN caution has not been followed up. The US Ambassador to Japan, Mike Mansfield, was a strong advocate of a US–Japan FTA in the later years of the Reagan administration, but the Japanese government was non-committal and the Bush administration has not pursued the idea.

Western Europe

The West Europeans withdrew from Pacific Asia in the post-war decades not just politically and militarily, but also economically. This meant that the EC was shielded longer than the United

States from the export expansion first of Japan and then of the NIEs, but it also missed out on significant opportunities.

In terms of total EC trade, Pacific Asia still holds a relatively small share. Even Japan in 1989 accounted for only about 4 per cent of total EC imports and 2 per cent of EC exports. The other nine Asian states together accounted for only 4 per cent of EC imports and 3 per cent of EC exports. It is the concentration, therefore, of Pacific Asian manufactured products in a few sectors which has disturbed the Europeans, for whom the rapid rise in market share in the late 1980s by consumer electronics and household appliances from South Korea and Taiwan suggested an ominous replay of Japan in the late 1970s. Although the ASEAN countries, including Singapore, benefit from some degree of favourable treatment through the EC–ASEAN Cooperation Agreement and the Generalized System of Preferences (GSP), South Korea and Taiwan do not have any such cooperative arrangement with the EC. It is these two, in particular, that have been seen as 'second Japans', and that have been increasingly subjected to the kinds of 'voluntary' export restraints (VERs) and anti-dumping actions that the EC already operates in respect of Japanese goods.[15] There is, therefore, a widespread suspicion in Pacific Asia that the EC's moves towards a single market by 1992 will merely increase protectionist tendencies.

From the viewpoint of the Pacific Asian countries, the EC declined slowly in significance as a trading partner through the 1970s and early 1980s. Its share of total Pacific Asian trade has now stabilized at around 11 per cent for both exports and imports. In the 1970s a combination of inward-looking policies as the EC enlarged, preoccupation with oil-related Middle Eastern trade, and generally low growth rates made the EC a less attractive trade partner than the United States. However, the general Pacific Asian desire for trade diversification mentioned earlier, together with signs of renewed economic vigour in Western Europe and market saturation in the United States, could lead to a rapid growth in EC–Pacific Asia trade in the 1990s. Whether or not this happens depends largely on the degree of EC openness after 1992.

The EC's rather dismal record on trade is repeated in FDI into the region. Japan and the United States are well ahead of the EC, which has dropped from providing 15 per cent of annual inflows during the 1950–70 period to roughly 10 per cent of annual flows throughout the 1980s. In terms of cumulative amounts, at the end of 1986 (see Table 6), only in Malaysia and Singapore was it the largest foreign investor – and that status was a reflection more of past British investment than of fresh flows of FDI into this rapidly growing region.

Investment flows have been growing in the other direction. The EC's moves towards the 1992 single market have accentuated the growing trend during the 1980s for the Pacific Asian countries to invest in the EC. This new investment has come predominantly from Japan, which by March 1990 had invested a total of US $41 billion in the EC, $14 billion of which was invested in FY 1989 alone. Over one-third of the cumulative total has gone into Britain. Again following in Japan's footsteps, South Korea, and to a far lesser extent Taiwan, have begun since the mid-1980s to set up manufacturing plants and financial operations inside the EC.

The European record on ODA has been more encouraging than on trade and investment. The EC countries have provided more bilateral aid than the US throughout the 1980s, and for the year 1986 the EC briefly topped Japan as the largest aid donor to Indonesia and Malaysia.

CHINA

The process of reform and modernization that started in China in 1978 has inevitably had an impact on regional economic patterns. Although this raised fears that low-cost competition would undercut other Pacific Asian producers, it also opened up promising possibilities for new cooperative arrangements, especially through the relocation of manufacturing operations from other countries in the region.

China's foreign trade has been growing rapidly during the 1980s, but it has been characterized by severe fluctuations from surplus to deficit and back again. Manufactures, mainly textiles, contribute just over half of total exports; China's main export market is Japan, which purchased about 16 per cent of its exports in 1989, with the US and the EC taking about 9 per cent each. Textile exports have been the greatest growth area, and it is now the largest single supplier of textile and clothing imports to the United States. In response, the United States has been negotiating a limit to the growth of textile imports from China. Japan is its leading supplier of manufactured goods, followed by the EC, US and Hong Kong. China is increasingly an important importer from the NIEs and Japan, especially of intermediate goods, machinery and equipment as well as services, which is partly explained by new FDI flows into China. Trade with both South Korea and Taiwan has increased rapidly over the 1986–9 period.

Despite the events in China of May–June 1989, its participation in regional trade and investment is likely to continue to expand in the 1990s (even with Western partners, it is only investment into, rather than trade with, China which has suffered). The real limitation on its role as a regional partner is the fact that it is a very poor country with vast needs for investment in domestic infrastructure. Yet, at the fringes, there are signs of a more important role to come. In the second half of the 1980s it became the host for the relocation of labour-intensive production from the NIEs, especially from Hong Kong, but increasingly from Taiwan and South Korea as well. The 1988 Sino-Japanese investment protection agreement was aimed at consolidating a permanent address for Japanese capital in China's coastal region. From this FDI China gets some technology transfer, employment creation, manufacturing and product promotion. It has also been an important recipient of ODA from Japan and other OECD countries – to the extent that some ASEAN countries have feared being crowded out of this kind of assistance.

CONCLUSIONS

The three dominant economic linkages that have been examined in this chapter – trade flows, foreign direct investment and bilateral aid – show some complex patterns of interdependence, both within and beyond the Pacific Asian region. The 1980s saw a major increase in the *absolute* size of trade, aid and FDI flows in the region, which is one possible definition of economic interdependence. These flows also grew in *relative* terms for most of the countries of the region: that is, as a proportion of their GDPs. This constitutes another possible definition of interdependence.

If, however, the test of growing regional interdependence is an increase in the *share* of external flows (i.e. trade, FDI and aid) that take place *within* the region, then the data for 1980–9, as a whole, do not support such a hypothesis. The picture is, in fact, more complicated than that. Trade by Japan, the NIEs and the ASEAN countries has, in all three cases, grown faster during the 1980s with extra-regional partners (in particular, the United

States) than with regional partners. For the NIEs a relative increase in regional trade importance began to show only in 1987, whereas the ASEAN-5 were actually showing a relative decrease in regional trade importance at this time. Nevertheless, the data do show a significantly increased reliance by the ASEAN-5 on trade with the four NIEs, and a relative increase of trade intensity by the NIEs with Japan (and, even more clearly, with China) during the 1980s. Given the very fast growth rates of many of these countries, this may be an important indicator of future trends. The opening of the Japanese market, in particular, is important in the NIEs' attempts to diversify their markets, and could have far-reaching effects on regional trade.

On the investment side, Japanese and NIE FDI has gone predominantly to the US and other countries outside the region (the 1992 process in Europe may well accentuate this trend); this is not just to beat perceived protectionism, but reflects a genuine pull from these countries. Nevertheless, FDI flows from Japan to the NIEs, and from both into ASEAN, are playing an increasingly important role in spreading technology, capital and marketing expertise in the region, and providing a new spur to intra-regional trade. There is evidence of new factor movements, and an increasingly specialized and complementary division of labour within the region. For ASEAN especially, these flows are large in relation to the home economies.

As far as the poorer countries of the region are concerned, Japan increasingly dominates as the major aid donor. As Japan expands its total aid budget, China and other low-income countries can expect to reap economic benefits from Japan's regional interests. The role of South Korea and Taiwan as regional donors is also expanding, and may be closely related, as is Japan's aid, to FDI expansion in the region.

The picture of the early and mid-1980s is therefore one of growing global – rather than merely regional – economic integration and interdependence. But the regional changes that began to be seen in the late 1980s, often closely associated with FDI flows, suggest that the 1990s will see an even more complex network of economic interactions. Inevitably, such heightened economic interplay will not be without political repercussions – both domestic and external.

Chapter 2

The security context
Region in flux

The Pacific Asian security environment presents a complex web of power relationships, with an increasingly diversified cast of players acting out the competition for power and influence. Moreover, there is no one common perception of 'threat', and national security issues relate not only to external aggression but also, if not more so, to domestic developments. The fragility of political regimes, the challenges to state- and nation-building, and the obstacles to democratization in Pacific Asia – all can lead to instability.

Paradoxically, despite being seen as a region of political turmoil, and despite the huge build-up of military forces, American, Soviet and Chinese, Pacific Asia has seemed to be supplementary – rather than pivotal – to Western security interests. It has served, in effect, as a testing-ground for the cold war: it has provided a context both for real East–West confrontation, such as occurred in the Korean war (1950–3), and for the ideological battle of wills, as exemplified in the second Indochinese war (c. 1964–75).

As noted in Chapter 1, it was the US security umbrella that enabled fledgling political regimes to survive, and then to succeed in economic terms. Now, however, the emphasis has shifted. The withdrawal of American forces is already under way; the question is merely whether the US military presence will be reduced gradually or precipitately.[1]

In future, the role of the United States will relate not to its strength in terms of numbers, but to its ability, in a qualitative sense, to offer a credible response to any threat that might occur. American forces, therefore, need to be disposed in such a way as to allow the United States to continue to project its power throughout the region despite the reduction in force levels. As the Korean and Vietnamese experiences have shown, its aerial and maritime capabilities are its greatest strengths,[2] and it is on these two factors – and how they translate in political terms – that the effectiveness of a reduced US presence will hinge. In a word, the issue for the future is one of credibility.

The Soviet Union, similarly, has been adjusting its stance. The 1986 Vladivostok, and the 1988 Krasnoyarsk, speeches of President Mikhail Gorbachev marked a new phase in Soviet strategy. They signalled the Soviet desire to compete with the United States in the region under a new set of rules, one in which priority would be given to political and economic factors, rather than to ideology and military strength as formerly.[3] US–Soviet competition – in the regional setting as in the global – will continue in the 1990s, but the ground rules are being rewritten.

The complexity of the region's security environment derives from the multiplicity of interactions that are going on at the same time but at different levels. On one level are the superpowers; below them, other major military powers, such as Japan and China (and one could include India), whose interactions in the region are increasing; and, finally, various smaller, or 'middle', powers, with numerically substantial armies (Vietnam and the two Koreas being the main ones), or aspiring roles (Indonesia being the prime example), also contend in sub-regional contexts. As in the European theatre, so potentially in Pacific Asia, superpower confrontation is likely to be replaced by other tensions, some of them resurgent ambitions that were previously contained by, or subsumed in, the dominant cold-war pattern. This chapter will look, in turn, at the roles of the superpowers; at those of China and Japan; at some of the disputes occurring between smaller powers; and, finally, at arms control and possible new security structures for the 1990s.

THE US/SOVIET POWER EQUATION

From the late 1940s through to the 1980s, the US security role in Pacific Asia was based on a policy of containment of communism – not just by military means, but also by means of political and economic measures, as part of a comprehensive and tenacious approach. Although the record of the United States was impressive, the Vietnam experience showed that its success was not inevitable, particularly where the appeal of nationalism and self-determination (rather than communism *per se*) was strong. The threat to its hegemony, moreover, took several forms, as the pattern of inter-state relations shifted: first a combined Soviet–Chinese challenge (up to 1959–60); then twin but separate threats from the Soviet Union and China (up to the mid-1970s); and finally a period of Sino-American rapprochement and the larger threat of Soviet expansionism through the 1980s. In the 1990s, the nature of the communist challenge will become even more varied, as the communist world itself becomes more pluralistic and its ideological fervour less marked.

From the viewpoint of the United States, therefore, containing Soviet influence is now only one of its major challenges in the region; the full range of its interests is outlined in a Department of Defense report of April 1990:

> Despite the decade of change that we see, our regional interests in Asia will remain similar to those we have pursued in the past: protecting the United States from attack; supporting our global deterrence policy; preserving our political and economic access; maintaining the balance of power to prevent the rise of any regional hegemony; strengthening the Western orientation of the Asian nations; fostering the growth of democracy and human rights; deterring nuclear proliferation; and ensuring freedom of navigation. The principal elements of our Asian strategy – forward-deployed forces, overseas bases, and bilateral security arrangements – will remain valid and essential to maintaining regional stability, deterring aggression, and preserving US interests.[4]

From a strategic perspective, Pacific Asia presents two main problems: a vast maritime area (involving aerial cover) and a land mass displaying serious logistical difficulties. These military challenges are compounded by the region's political complexities. US ground troops in the Pacific theatre are greatly outnumbered by those of potential adversaries (the Soviet Union, China, Vietnam). In the 1990s, in the light of budgetary constraints and reduced threat perceptions, the Pentagon envisages a phased reduction of forward-deployed US forces by 14,000–15,000 men over three years from the 1990 total of 135,000.[5] After that, phased force reductions will be adjusted according to the prevailing circumstances; at the same time, the USA's allies will be expected to take greater responsibility for their own defence in terms of cost-sharing and additional operational roles.[6] When one looks at the approximate military balance between the United States and the Soviet Union in the second half of the 1980s (Table 9), it is clear that Soviet forces had an overwhelming numerical advantage, although it could be argued that they were largely concentrated along the Sino-Soviet border. Following Gorbachev's December 1988 and May 1989 announcements of unilateral troop reductions, cuts have been made in Soviet forces in Mongolia and on the Sino-Soviet border, but the levels on the Pacific seaboard have remained steady. This supports the theory that the US war-fighting strategy rests not on numbers, but on the quality of men, and on firepower (especially from the air), tactical superiority and easily available reinforcements.

Table 9 US–Soviet military balance in East Asia and the Pacific in the 1980s, selected data

	United States		Soviet Union	
	1983	1985*	1983	1989–90
Divisions	4	4	35	50
Tanks	325	325	9,000	11,500
Bombers	14	14	435	215
Tactical aircraft	750	832	1,565	890
Naval aircraft	108	117	50	245

Sources: As cited in Young Whan Kihl and Lawrence Grinter (eds.), *Asian-Pacific Security: Emerging Challenges and Responses* (New Delhi: Archives Publishers for Lynne Rienner, 1987), p. 8; John M. Collins, *US–Soviet Military Balance, 1980–85* (Washington: Pergamon/Brassey's, 1985), pp. 272–3; International Institute for Strategic Studies, *The Military Balance, 1989–90* (London: Brassey's for IISS, 1990), pp. 41–2; US Department of Defense, *A Strategic Framework for the Asian Pacific Rim: Looking Toward the 21st Century*, Report to the US Congress, April 1990, p. 5.

*The 1985 figures are drawn from Collins, as cited. The figures for 1989–90 can be assumed to be similar (although, except in the case of divisions, they may be slightly lower, since there has probably been a 'build-down').

In the maritime dimension, too, the quantitative edge seems to lie with the Soviet Union. As shown in Table 10, the total number of Soviet ships was more than four times the US total in 1989–90, a lead that had been increasing right through the 1980s. However, the qualitative edge again lies with the United States. Thus, in 1989, the United States had considerably more surface combat vessels than the Soviet Union; moreover, it has seven aircraft carriers in the Pacific, which helped to pack in an awesome naval and aerial capacity that the Soviets simply cannot match. Impressive as the Soviet Union's naval build-up has been, it is hampered by its lack of bases outside the Soviet Far East (its facilities in Vietnam and Cambodia are now being less utilized), a weak air-defence system, and submarines that are inferior to those of the United States.[7] The US naval advantages have made it a top Soviet concern to press for naval arms control in the Pacific, but these overtures have been flatly rejected by Washington.

Table 10 General comparison of US and Soviet naval forces in Pacific Asia, selected years

	1968		1973		1984–5		1989–90*	
	US	SU	US	SU	US	SU	US	SU
Ships total	427	660	277	646	213	808	191	875
Carriers	11	0	8	0	6	2	7	2
Surface combatants	140	55	104	60	92	88	100	75
Submarines (general-purpose)†	59	95	47	90	40	95	43	96
Submarines (SSBN)	7	10	9	20	3	31	8	24
Amphibious	97	0	41	4	32	22	33	21

Sources: D. C. Daniel and G. D. Tarleton, 'The US Navy in the Western-Pacific', *Asia Pacific Community* (Winter, 1986), p. 119; International Institute for Strategic Studies, *The Military Balance, 1989–90* (London: Brassey's for the IISS), p. 26, p. 42; US Department of Defense, *A Strategic Framework for the Asian Pacific Rim: Looking Toward the 21st Century*, Report to the US Congress, April 1990, p. 5.

*The 'Ships total' figure for the Soviets includes all ships in the Soviet Pacific Command, obtained from the US Department of Defense, as cited below.

†Includes nuclear-powered.

An important issue relating to US maritime power is that of the on-shore infrastructure facilities for the forward-deployed naval forces. The question, for the 1990s, is whether the US military presence will be impaired by the return of the Subic Bay naval facilities, and the Clark airfield facilities, to the Philippine authorities. Although alternative arrangements are being discussed (potentially, expanded access in Singapore, Brunei, Guam or New Zealand), the impairment may be logistical rather than operational in view of the technological and firepower edge of the US navy.

In 1980, the US Commander-in-Chief of the Pacific, Admiral

Long, regarded the margin in Pacific Asia between the US and Soviet armed forces as 'too close to call';[8] in the early 1990s, the United States should probably be seen as being, operationally, in the ascendant. More important than military capabilities, however, may be the political will of the United States to continue to play a leading strategic role, and the effect of any perceived lessening of its interests.

THE 'DECLINE' OF THE UNITED STATES?

From the mid-1940s onwards, US hegemony was a fact of the Pacific Asian politico-military setting, even though it did not always seem an unassailable position.

From 1975 onwards, however, as a result of the US defeat in Vietnam, a 'withdrawal syndrome' became apparent, although in practice the military superiority of the United States remained intact, notwithstanding a gradual reduction of troop strength. The perception in the region of US military might and superiority has remained similarly intact.[9] Instead doubts have emerged about the strength of the US *political* commitment.

Since the mid-1980s, the USA's main preoccupations have been its twin budget and trade deficits, and its seeming lack of ability to sustain itself as both a military and a techno-industrial power. But the notion of the 'decline' of the United States is more a manifestation of fashionable debate than a reality.[10] Whatever may be said about a reduced lead in technological and economic strength, the impact of the United States on the international economy, and its own continued potential for growth, have been amply demonstrated in the post-Vietnam era.[11] The decline is only relative. More to the point is whether it still has what former President Nixon referred to in 1987 as 'the will to power'.[12] Therefore, the manner in which the United States responds over the coming months to the current crisis in the Gulf will have implications that extend far beyond the crisis itself, and will have a profound effect on the future security of the Pacific Asian region.

THE NEW SOVIET UNION

From the late 1970s onwards, the Soviet Union's military build-up of naval strength in the Pacific, its invasion of Afghanistan, its close alliance with India (acting as its principal supplier of arms), its access to bases at Cam Ranh and Da Nang in Vietnam (and also as the main supplier of aid to Vietnam), the strengthening of its garrisons in the disputed Northern Territories, and its 'fishing' forays in the South Pacific were all viewed as a clear indication of the Soviet challenge to US military hegemony. Gorbachev's arrival on the scene, armed only with peace initiatives, therefore startled the entire international community. The Soviet Union's objectives were, however, subject to varying interpretation, ranging from acquiescence in the changing structure of power in the world and in the Pacific, and hence acceptance of its right to be a 'new boy on the block', to cynicism (the Chinese and Japanese, for example, looking for 'actions, not words'), to fear of a possible *Pax Sovietica* if the United States slipped from its dominant position.[13]

But Soviet 'words' were, in fact, backed up by actions, a series of bold initiatives being taken throughout the late 1980s – the withdrawal from Afghanistan, increasing dialogue with the Japanese, a partial reduction in Soviet ships and aircraft based in Vietnam, participation in the 1988 Seoul Olympics, leading to the recognition of South Korea in September 1990, involvement in the Pacific Economic Cooperation Conference (PECC), diplomatic and trade agreements with many Pacific Asian countries, and the near-achievement of friendly relations with China, leading to the Sino-Soviet summit of May 1989. Whereas proposals for a region-wide collective security system had fallen on deaf ears in the pre-Gorbachev era, Soviet support for a denuclearized Pacific Asia now lent some basis to the ASEAN proposal – pushed largely by Indonesia and Malaysia – for a 'Nuclear-Weapons-Free Zone' (NWFZ) in Southeast Asia. Although the Soviets have had less success with their Vietnamese allies on the Cambodian question (not so much in terms of Vietnamese troop withdrawals as in terms of a failure to resolve the internal power-struggles of the Cambodian factions), their initiatives have been generally welcomed by the countries in the region.

These efforts have helped to make it more likely that the Soviet Union will be viewed as a legitimate power in the region, one that can be accepted in the international system. Moreover, during 1990, internal economic and political pressures (threatening even disintegration) made a Soviet offensive, either military or ideological, more and more unlikely.

CHINA

Soviet and Chinese officials played down the significance of the May 1989 summit between Comrades Gorbachev and Deng in Beijing, alluding to it more as a 'symbolic' affirmation of their closer ties after some 30 years of rivalry and hostility. Certainly it was not a return to the close alliance of the 1950s. The summit made it plain, moreover, that, from the Chinese perspective, considerable differences remain as to the extent of the Vietnamese troop pull-out and the nature of the Kampuchea solution, so that the summit did not lead, in effect, to a Sino-Soviet accord superimposed on this Southeast Asian tragedy.[14] It did represent, nevertheless, a significant gain for both sides, in that both needed to have a peaceful regional environment in order to concentrate on domestic economic reconstruction; the logic of Pacific Asian developmentalism pushed them closer together.

Above all, the Gorbachev–Deng summit highlighted the declining importance of ideology in world politics. The point was made explicitly by Gorbachev when he remarked on his China visit that the challenge of Marxism is to adapt itself to a world very different from the one that its founder had known. It was no coincidence that the summit took place when both countries were grappling with political and economic reforms while, at the same time, still wanting to remain basically socialist. Both have been trying to deal with the same question: is there a half-way house between socialism and capitalism? Having put ideology on hold while keeping the party's role intact, both Deng and Gorbachev may have felt that their respective strengths could grow only if they paid attention to the seemingly inevitable forces of socio-economic modernization. However, since mid-1989 and the massacre in Beijing's Tiananmen Square, their responses have become increasingly divergent. In contrast with China's post-Tiananmen caution and ambivalence, the Soviet Union is undergoing change at breakneck pace with a radical programme of decentralization and deregulation of economic (and, by inevitable extension, political) decision-making.

The two states also have a tacit interest in promoting regional stability (both have moved towards closer contact with South Korea and a rebalancing of their interests on the Korean peninsula, for example) and are looking for economic advantage, not just through increasing their bilateral trade but also by involving

Pacific Asian capitalist neighbours in potential multinational joint ventures. For the countries of Pacific Asia, the military dangers of communism are gone. But the Soviet and Chinese efforts at modernization – whether they succeed or whether they fail – could present dangers that are harder to anticipate and equally difficult to contend with.

China will continue its 'independent' actions, such as developing its strategic nuclear weapons at the same time as it slims down and modernizes its conventional forces, expanding its naval capabilities, continuing its arms sales to developing countries (China is now the fifth largest arms exporter), and endeavouring to play a role in regional disputes, such as Cambodia. It will be a wary actor, and will avoid exerting too active a role in the region until it achieves a sufficient degree of economic and military modernization. Since the massacre in Tiananmen Square, the initial tendencies to isolate China – never as strong in the region as in the West – have given way to a desire to draw China in, in constructive engagement. By the autumn of 1990, while the Chinese military authorities were still preoccupied with domestic political issues, China's external situation in the region appeared increasingly peaceful. Not only had relations been improved with neighbours such as the Soviet Union, India and even Vietnam, but Indonesia and Singapore had established diplomatic relations.

A HEIGHTENED DEFENCE ROLE FOR JAPAN

The August 1990 Gulf crisis, and the subsequent attempts of the Japanese to pass new legislation to enable their Self-Defence Forces (SDF) to cooperate in UN peace-keeping activities, have reopened with a vengeance the internal and external debate about Japan's role in the region's security framework. Clearly the Japanese are not prepared to play too assertive a role, and the reigning domestic 'no-war' attitude, which sees Japan as closely tied to US leadership in security and defence, will mean it will work in tandem with others. Domestic opposition, as well as the concern publicly expressed by neighbouring Pacific Asian countries, will act as constraints on the SDF's participation in UN peace-keeping activities, let alone in more active regional security contexts.

Japan's security structure has been based on the twin supports of the revised Japan–US Security Treaty (1960) and the growing strength of the Self-Defence Forces. With the relative decline of the USA's economic and political strength in the 1970s and 1980s, pressure on Japan to share the burden of regional security has grown. In the absence of any clearly defined goals of its own, Japan's internal debates over defence have usually been cast in terms of accommodating the United States.

Measured in US dollars, Japanese defence spending is the third highest in the world (although its climb up the table has been aided by the turnaround in the yen/dollar exchange rate), and it is equal to that of all the other Pacific Asian countries combined.[15] Yet much of the budget goes on personnel and pensions costs; the land SDF are favoured at the expense of the naval and air arms; weapons procurement programmes are running about four years behind schedule; and, despite the claims made in 1983 by Prime Minister Nakasone Yasuhiro that Japan was an 'unsinkable air-craft carrier', there are still doubts about its ability to defend either itself or its sea lanes.

Moreover, despite all its talk about burden-sharing, the United States is unlikely to choose to abrogate its role as a Pacific power and allow Japan to be its surrogate. What is more likely for the 1990s is that the security environment will be seen in joint-leader-ship terms, but in a partnership in which the US role will be primary and that of Japan secondary and supportive. Similarly, Japan will continue to remain outside any broader formal Western or regional security alliances. Although the Japanese have been participating since 1980 in the Rimpac (Rim of the Pacific) naval exercises, held every two years, with US, Canadian, Australian and, occasionally, British warships, they are not involved directly in NATO activities or in bilateral military exercises with any Pacific Asian nation. A call, in May 1990, by Thai Prime Minister Chatichai Choonhavan for joint maritime exercises between Japan and Thailand received no positive support either from Japan or from other ASEAN partners.[16]

REGIONAL DISPUTES

A notable feature of the Pacific Asian security context has been the high incidence of local or low-intensity conflict. This type of conflict often has an ideological content, which, as in the 1978 Vietnamese invasion of Kampuchea and the subsequent Kampu-chean resistance to the Phnom Penh regime, may include a signifi-cant element of power rivalry, in that the ideological schisms are *internal*. Low-intensity conflict is an intra-national perpetration of armed violence with political objectives: that is, insurgency or civil war. Over time, governments in the region have overcome insurgencies by acquiring legitimacy through effective authority; in Malaysia, the final surrender of the Malayan Communist Party in December 1989 is an example. Conversely, the communist insurgency in the Philippines will continue to cause serious problems to the Aquino government as the government's authority comes under increasing challenge from all sides. The Philippines will remain the most fragile and volatile state in Pacific Asia for some time to come, and, as such, it will have the potential for disturbing the regional order, not just as a result of an early departure of US forces from the bases there, but also through the destabilization and incapacitation of an ASEAN founder-member.

Apart from the Philippines, two other areas remain at the centre of regional security concerns: Cambodia and the Korean peninsula. Both have seemed intractable disputes – one a lengthy and bloody civil war, the other a prolonged and chilly state of neither war nor peace – yet both are beginning to show some signs of winding down, not least as the superpowers, and the major powers, act more flexibly in trying to shift the established positions of local participants.

War seems to have been going on in Indochina virtually uninterrupted since 1941; Cambodia is now left as the final tragedy. The Soviets have played both a direct and an indirect role in trying to bring peace to the area: direct, by encouraging the Vietnamese withdrawal of forces from Cambodia in 1989; and, indirect, by reassuring China (now less fearful of Soviet encirclement following the marked reduction of Soviet forces at the Can Ramh Bay base in Vietnam) and by cutting back on its economic assistance so as to force Vietnam to be more flexible politically. In the West, the Cambodian situation, an outgrowth of the Vietnam war, has often been viewed as part of the US legacy in Southeast Asia; however, despite the US change of policy towards Vietnamese and Cambodian representation in August 1990, the US role is now only marginal. The resolution of the crisis now depends much more on the direct backers of the feuding Cambodian parties, China and Vietnam, and ultimately on the Cambodian leaders themselves.

Over the years, many countries have tried to bring peace to Cambodia. Since 1988 Indonesia has organized a series of meetings known as the Jakarta Informal Meetings, involving the main regional parties; in 1989 France organized an international conference, and in June 1990 Japan organized a conference of the Cambodian factions. These attempts all failed because of a lack of agreement on the form that a transitional government of Cambodia, pending free elections, should take, and whether the Khmer Rouge should be involved in it. Given the relative military strengths of the warring Cambodian groups, a role in any interim administration for the Khmer Rouge will be hard to avoid, but there is considerable distaste among external powers for a return of Pol Pot and his close colleagues.

In September 1990, however, the four Cambodian factions (the Khmer Rouge, the two non-communist resistance groups and the Phnom Penh government) agreed in principle to a plan worked out by the UN Security Council for the formation of a Supreme National Council (SNC) as the centre-piece of the proposed UN interim administration.[17] However, no agreement could be reached among the SNC members on electing Prince Sihanouk, the resistance leader, as head, and the talks subsequently broke down. Both China, wishing to eliminate its international pariah status, and Vietnam, aware that Cambodia is the key to unlocking the US-led embargo against it, have acted more flexibly during 1990 and brought greater pressure to bear on their protégés, the Khmer Rouge and the Phnom Penh government respectively. Nevertheless, by the end of the year, it was clear that the Cambodian problem remained both tortuous and one where the role of regional actors would be central.

Whereas Cambodia can be characterized as a continuing, if declining, 'hot' war, the Korean peninsula represents a different security challenge – a 'cold' war which may gradually be beginning to thaw. A Korean proverb describes Korea as a prawn, whose back is liable to be broken by the convulsions of the neighbouring great-power whales. For the past four decades, there have been two half-prawns and at least four whales interested. The pace of reconciliation between the two Koreas has been affected not just by the lack of mutual trust and divergent priorities between them but also by the attitude of the four major external powers, which, until recently, have been reluctant, to a lesser or greater degree, to upset the *status quo* on the peninsula.

Relations between the two Koreas remain tense, with the elements of economic, diplomatic and military competition between the two still paramount. The military balance, although characterized by a continuing build-up and modernization, is actually relatively stable. The quantitative edge in both men and weaponry lies with the North, but qualitatively the South is ahead; given the greater budgetary expenditure in the South over the past fifteen years, the South is getting closer to military parity with the North.[18] South Korean defence officials still consider that parity will be achieved early next century, but the Bush administration argues that the mid-1990s is more likely. Concern has been expressed recently about North Korea's potential for acquiring or producing nuclear weapons, but the Soviets – suppliers of North Korea's nuclear technology – are keen to prevent nuclear weapon proliferation in the area. Nevertheless, Korea remains a potential military flashpoint, even though none of the superpowers or major powers has an interest in further conflict there.

The security framework of the Korean peninsula has to be seen on two levels: relations between the 'whales' themselves and with the two Koreas, and relations between the two Koreas themselves. Neither level can be completely divorced from the other. External change, primarily the Sino-US rapprochement, first brought the two Koreas into negotiations in 1972, for example; Sino-Soviet rapprochement in 1989 reduced North Korean leverage over its two allies and made it turn towards the South and its allies. Since 1988, as symbolized by Soviet and Chinese participation in the Seoul Olympics, the environment has changed. First, South Korea has developed economic and political contacts with the Soviet Union and China, culminating in the Soviet Union's recognition of South Korea in September 1990 and the Chinese agreement to exchange trade offices the following month.[19] Second, North Korea has begun, tentatively, to try to move out of its international isolation, by carrying on intermittent discussions with US diplomats, in Beijing, and by trying to push Japan into establishing diplomatic relations.[20]

Although North Korea still publicly rejects the notion of 'cross-recognition' and 'two Koreas', in practice these new contacts herald a move towards acceptance by all the surrounding major powers of the realities of a divided peninsula. However, once again, only the Koreans themselves can move towards peace, and at present, despite meetings between the two prime ministers at the end of 1990, there is little real evidence of a meeting of minds. Nevertheless, the fact that these unprecedented meetings at the very top level took place at all suggests at least the potential for a new détente. Some kind of tension-reducing measures could in due course lead to reconciliation and a measure of arms control and graded force reductions, even if the prospect of German-style reunification still remains distant.

Finally, the 1990s are likely to intensify a more recent regional security challenge: the management of convergent interests both in the South China Sea and in the waters of Northeast Asia.[21] Traditionally, the regional waters served as a thoroughfare for trade and cultural influence, but in recent years, although commercial traffic is still important, local and regional competition over territorial claims to islands and sea space, enhanced by overlapping jurisdictions of maritime exclusive economic zones and continental-shelf zones, has grown. Potential oil and other natural-resource deposits are one factor, but so too are the strategic positions of the various small islands that straddle vital sea-zones. These offshore claims are made more volatile by enhanced military capabilities and the willingness of some states to support their claims by using force, such as China's March 1988 actions in the Spratly islands.[22] Even where competing claims appear to have been shelved for the distant future, the potential for trouble exists, as shown in the autumn of 1990, when the dormant claims of Japan, China and Taiwan to the Senkaku islands were awakened by the activities of a small Japanese ultra-nationalist group. The need to develop a framework to avoid military clashes and to assist in the peaceful exploration of resources in these areas will become increasingly important in the coming decade.

ARMS CONTROL AND NEW SECURITY STRUCTURES

Pacific Asia does not have a tradition of arms control, and the record of worthwhile and effective measures is still meagre by comparison with that in Europe.[23] Of course, some arms control agreements at the global level, such as the US-Soviet Treaty on Intermediate-range Nuclear Forces in 1988, do have an impact on the region (at Japanese and Chinese insistence it was made clear, for example, that Soviet SS-20 missiles would have to be dismantled rather than moved from the European to the Asian theatre). Certainly, US–Soviet bipolarity is giving way to a trend of global security interdependence and multipolarity.

Nevertheless, the absence in Pacific Asia of two generally homogeneous bloc systems, such as NATO and the Warsaw Pact in pre-1989 Europe, has meant that such arms control as took place tended to be unilateral, with very little being achieved by way of bilateral or multilateral agreements. In the late 1980s, for example, both Soviet and Chinese force reductions emerged as unilateral gestures, although they both derived from and impacted on the developing Sino-Soviet rapprochement. The Bush administration's cutbacks announced in early 1990 would also fall into this category, and so, too, after failed negotiations multilaterally, would the Vietnamese withdrawal from Cambodia in 1989. Formal negotiations have had a poor success rate; proposals have abounded, but few have been realistic. For example, according to statistics issued by the South Korean National Unification Board, there have been a total of 294 proposals on military questions exchanged between North and South Korea between 1945 and 1988, without one bearing fruit.[24]

The intense debate going on within Europe about creating a new political and security framework, revolving primarily around a redefined role for the Conference on Security and Cooperation in Europe (CSCE), has provoked a new debate in Pacific Asia about regional security systems. Multilateral alliances have tended not to last in this part of the world. The main US-convened alliances, products of the cold war – the Asia–Pacific Council (ASPAC), the Southeast Asia Treaty Organization (SEATO) and even ANZUS (Australia, New Zealand and the United States) – have become defunct or virtually unworkable. Although there was some talk of expanding the Five-Power Defence Arrangement (1970) to include Brunei (and even Indonesia and Thailand), that treaty too has become semi-dormant. Bilateral alliances, both between the United States and its regional allies and between China and the Soviet Union and some fellow socialist countries, have displayed better staying-power. Now, however, the emphasis is beginning to turn back to multilateral frameworks that might encompass all ideological viewpoints.

Since 1969, successive Soviet leaders, including Gorbachev at Krasnoyarsk in 1988, have floated ideas for a regional security organization, but with generally negative responses from the region. However, in 1990, there seemed to be a surge in interest, not least because of the European precedent. In July 1990 the Canadian Foreign Minister, Joe Clark, took the initiative in proposing a CSCE-type security organization that would cover confidence-building measures; and in September Soviet Foreign

Minister Eduard Shevardnadze put forward proposals for an Asian Foreign Ministers' Conference to consider the creation of a security organization.[25] Proposals of this kind are subject to much less critical and suspicious scrutiny than formerly, but there are many countries in the region (including, notably, Japan) that are not yet convinced of the viability of a multilateral framework.

INTO THE 1990s

A region in flux, in which US military power is no longer predominant, may well be the security scenario of the 1990s. The uncertainties, trends and challenges of the decade are well summarized by the US government itself:

> Political volatility and turbulence will characterize key countries – China, the Soviet Union, North Korea, Cambodia and the Philippines, to name a few. Political uncertainties are exacerbated by the major changes in generational leadership that will occur, such as in China, North Korea, Singapore, Vietnam and Indonesia. Intensified economic competition within the region and with the United States will increasingly complicate security relationships. Moscow will undoubtedly be a more active player in the Asian diplomatic arena as it seeks to further mend ties with Beijing and obtain financial and technological aid from Japan and South Korea. Overall, for the United States, the decade will present opportunities, and important challenges: maintaining our security arrangements; meeting stiff technological and economic competition; containing Soviet influence; and managing, with fewer resources, the process of change.[26]

Managing the process of change in a world of greater economic and political interdependence will present challenges to Pacific Asian security that are different from those of the era of clear US hegemony. One can expect the 1990s to be a 'co-polar' world, in which US politico-military strength will be supported by Japanese economic power, even though the exact parameters of this partnership will not always be clear-cut or immutable.

Either an apparent decline in US military strength, or a lessening of the US commitment because of a perceived reduction in the rivalry of the Soviet Union, might result in a power vacuum in the region which other regional middle and major powers might attempt to fill – a fear expressed, for example, by one second-generation leader, Brigadier-General Lee Hsien Loong of Singapore.[27] However, barring some unforeseeable turn of events in, say, the Middle East, it is most unlikely that the United States will cease to be a Pacific power well into the twenty-first century. It will not relinquish that role, even though it may be forced, for economic reasons, to adjust it and to put more emphasis on burden-sharing.

Thus, in the 1990s, the resolution of many of the region's security tensions will depend to some extent on how US strength is rebalanced *vis-à-vis* other major powers. But trouble-spots will remain in Pacific Asia. It is to be hoped that the region's overriding commitment to economic growth will help it to avoid political follies.

Chapter 3
The developmental state
A tentative framework

The spectacular – and continued – economic growth of the Pacific Asian countries is almost taken for granted nowadays. Yet it is only since the late 1960s that the 'flying geese' of Pacific Asia started on their remarkable course. The late Herman Kahn,[1] and subsequently Ezra Vogel,[2] were among the first to draw attention to the implications of this phenomenon, with their appraisal of the rapid emergence of Japan as 'Number One' or 'superstate', and in its train the four NIEs of Pacific Asia – Hong Kong, Singapore, South Korea, and Taiwan. If a flying-geese pattern is broadly accepted as some kind of developmental path for the region, then the ASEAN countries (minus Singapore) should follow in the wake of Japan and the other 'new Japans'.

The most striking characteristic of the high-flyers of the region is their apparent ability to *sustain* economic growth. Thus, in the mid-1980s, after a downturn in performance resulting from the global recession, most Pacific Asian countries had, by 1987–8, resumed high growth. This recovery, it would seem, indicated the ability of these particular countries to adopt 'new approaches that emphasize the freeing of market forces through deregulation, privatization and the elimination of constraints on trade and investment'.[3] A few countries, however, proved to be less resilient, and the mid-1980s downturn revealed their vulnerability to international market forces even when adjustments were made.[4]

Even more significant were the effects of the mid-1980s recession on the politics and social stability of Pacific Asia's rapid-growth economies. The general unrest at this time demonstrated the perils of development in a context of global political and economic interdependence. The Honolulu-based East–West Center, in its 1987–8 Annual Report, rather tersely characterized the mid-1980s as a 'time of political turmoil' in Pacific Asia, and noted a 'region-wide crisis of political legitimacy' in the Philippines, China, South Korea, Malaysia – countries 'experiencing prolonged political struggles, the outcomes of which are not yet clear'.[5]

The correlation between economic growth and political change strikes at the very core of the developmental state model that is the theme of this chapter. One of the most prominent features of development in Pacific Asia is its high linkage to the rest of the world, resulting in what may be called 'development amid interdependence'. Indeed, the development which has taken place, and will continue to take place, would not be possible if it were not for the interdependence of the region with other regions. However, further development, in terms of changing patterns of interdependence, requires continual adjustment in both macro- and micro-economic terms.

This chapter will seek to determine whether there is a particular combination of factors, or set of conditions, that generally proves to be propitious for the creation, maintenance and continued growth of the Pacific Asian developmental state. In short, it will attempt the impossible: to build a model that might help the reader to interpret some of the material in this book. But first a brief word on the term 'developmentalism'.

We use the term 'developmentalism' – as opposed to 'development' or 'modernization' (with both of which it is roughly synonymous) – whenever we want to draw attention to two specifically Pacific Asian qualities: pragmatism and an emphasis on economic goals. Thus 'developmentalism' differs from 'development' in that the end-state of the latter may well be political and economic liberalism. Developmentalism, by contrast, is not rooted in any such ideological tradition, and the Western liberal-democratic state is hardly identifiable in Pacific Asia; indeed, it is probably not even recognized as a legitimate goal. Developmentalism in Pacific Asia is more a pragmatic policy choice, a concept designed to serve the purposes of state and, perhaps more crucially, regime survival. Or, to put it another way, developmentalism serves the purposes of state-building and state survival, rather than those of nation-building and national survival, even if the rhetoric of political leaders would suggest otherwise.

THE VARIABLES OF DEVELOPMENTALISM

Many people have wrestled with the problem of defining and explaining the tireless forward progression of the Pacific Asian economies. Lucian Pye, looking at Asia as a whole, describes it thus: 'The unity of Europe lies in its history; the unity of Asia is in the more subtle, but no less real, shared consciousness of the *desirability of change* and of making a future different from the past.[6] Some see Confucianism and the 'Eastern' values of thrift, diligence and selfless energy as being a primary cause for such phenomenal growth.[7] Others, such as Singapore's Lee Kuan Yew and Malaysia's Dr Mahathir Mohamad, less analytically, have simply exhorted their countrymen to emulate Japan, and more generally to 'look East' for models to follow. The difficulty, of course, is that there *is* no single model, or 'recipe', for the Pacific Asian success story. In the absence of any neat answers, let us examine five important recurring features, all amply illustrated in the chapters that follow.

(1) Strong government

The role of the state as the source, inspiration and expression of national development is unquestioned; indeed, strong government is seen as a substitute for effective political institutions. Whereas free enterprise appeared as a major characteristic of the economy, in reality the state has exercised an interventionist function as often as it deemed it necessary. The result is or was an Asian form of dirigisme in which the mix of the political and the economic functions is totally different from the experience of the West. If, in the West, 'that government governs best that governs least', the rule is turned on its head in the East to read, 'that government governs best that governs most'. East Asian publics, in this regard, may well be more susceptible to authoritarian rule; in a word, government, meaning state authority or regime, is expected to take charge.

Since government in the more dynamic Pacific Asian economies/ polities is regarded as benign, its legitimacy rests primarily on the regime's ability to achieve and sustain economic growth. It is perhaps useful at this point to distinguish 'states' and 'governments'.[8] States, as entities with corporate interests, are taken here to be more enduring than governments or regimes; however, governments in power behave as states. Furthermore, the role of regimes is to exercise power between states and societies. The relationship between regimes and states in fact provides useful clues as to whether developmentalism is going well or badly in Pacific Asian political systems. On the whole, the developmental exercise is state- or regime-driven, and more likely to succeed if the regime is non-communist or non-socialist. On the other hand, strong states with weak regimes or weak states with strong regimes are not likely to succeed.

Thus the political imperative of the 'developmental state' is *strong government*, whose mandate is to ensure the success of national development as a basis for the society's survival and future. In Pacific Asia, a form of government has arisen that, for want of a better label, may be called 'soft authoritarianism', a term that is applied only to the non-communist countries of the region.[9] Strong government leads to the assertion of authority to do what is necessary to achieve the state's goals of national development, and therefore the national or regime elites of these countries have little need for opposition or opposition groups. Democratic as Japan may be, it is difficult to refute the political supremacy of its Liberal Democratic Party, which has made possible the country's outstanding economic success. Political participation is allowed, but only to a limited extent, so that the resulting system may be termed 'semi-competitive politics'.

Except in Japan, political controls exercised over the population are pervasive, even when the country's political system may be described as stable; it is only recently that the political systems of South Korea and Taiwan have 'opened up'. However, there is a pronounced movement in this direction, since even in authoritarian Singapore, some members of the dominant ruling party have of late been pointing to the positive role that opposition groups can play in the political process. A *stable political system* has naturally been seen as the essential precondition of economic development, and clearly stability is also essential to these countries' security needs (in Taiwan and South Korea, the threat of invasion from mainland China and North Korea respectively; in Singapore, the danger of the violent overthrow of legitimate government by the communists or the more subtle menace of jealousy among its neighbouring Malay states). Circumstances in Japan are again rather different; but there, too, any prospect of instability in its political process would clearly be injurious to its comprehensive security (as discussed in Chapter 7), and in particular to its competitive ability in the predatory international environment.

It is therefore hardly surprising that *strong political parties* have emerged in the strong economies of Pacific Asia; where political parties were not prominent, their roles have been enacted by strong militaries and/or public bureaucracies. The role of political parties in this non-Western environment is not so much to represent the views of the public as to act as the vanguard of the government's policies and deeds, thereby causing the separation between state and party to become very blurred. The political party in power thus serves regime and state interests. The party's role has been either so dominant as to preclude the participation of other parties, or in fact is the manifestation of a one-party regime. In many cases, the party's function as a contestant for political power is as important as its mission to achieve economic development, both being viewed as crucial to the other. In other words, the dominant political parties have been agents of economic development, political power being expressed as the drive for national economic development.

A key role in the developmental polity has been played by *political personalities* and *modernizing elites*. It is difficult to imagine what would have happened in South Korea or Singapore had it not been for Park Chung-hee or Lee Kuan Yew. Nor can the role of Deng Xiaoping be discounted, as post-Mao China embarked on its long journey of the 'Four Modernizations'. In Taiwan, the ruling party's elites under Chiang father and son have been instrumental in pursuing economic goals that were politically, as well as economically, innovative, as in the land reform programme; and the subsequent 'reform from above' noted in Chapter 4 is another such example. But strong personal leaders do not always have the ability to spearhead economic development. In the case of the Philippines, it can be argued that although President Ferdinand Marcos was able to exert dictatorial control over his martial-law regime and 'new order' society, he was not able to achieve a level of economic development comparable with that of other high-growth Pacific Asian polities.

Finally, strong government assumes strong authority structures, in the form of *the bureaucracy, the police and the armed forces*. As noted, an effective public sector (which comprises the bureaucracy or civil service and para-bureaucratic organizations such as government enterprises and quasi-government agencies) is essential for economic growth. But in some Pacific Asian countries, such as South Korea, the mode of such governance has been so overpowering as to provoke the label 'bureaucratic authoritarianism'.[10] This implies the dominance of bureaucratic institutions at the expense of political organizations – clearly, an unhealthy situation.

In Pacific Asia in general, however, a strong bureaucracy is not regarded as going against the public interest. Indeed in Japan, according to Ezra Vogel, the public *expects* the bureaucracy to see to many of its needs.[11] Regimes intent on achieving economic development have of course seen the imperative of effective bureaucracies, and the bureaucracies themselves recognize the importance of pushing the growth process forward. The issue of the neutrality of public bureaucracies therefore did not arise in the high-growth polities of Pacific Asia, and in some respects their professionalism in performing their roles as technocrats was seen as part of their natural function. Indeed, at the topmost levels, the rapid turnover of personnel within the bureaucratic and political sectors, and in some cases in the business sectors as well, shows how interrelated these two elites – bureaucrats and technocrats – had become. Moreover, where military governments were in control, particular reliance was placed on such persons.

(2) Public/private sector relationship

Because of the stress on 'national' development, capital growth is encouraged for the purpose of enhancing the state and the nation; in other words, it has a nation-building function, and may perhaps be called 'neo-nationalistic' in aim. But it is a form of nation-building, or neo-nationalism, that has state and regime as its foci, even if these ends are pursued in the name of the nation. Similarly, the form of capitalism that has been encouraged in these societies could be called 'developmental capitalism'.

As Chapter 4 makes very clear, in examining the development strategies of the NIEs, the role of the private sector is not only looked upon favourably, but facilitated. In its highest form, a corporatist relationship between private and public sectors is formed, epitomized in what has been described as 'Japan Incorporated' and 'Singapore Incorporated'. Chalmers Johnson has elaborated on this phenomenon in his study of the role of Japan's Ministry of Trade and Industry (MITI) in fostering economic growth;[12] similar arguments can be made for the roles of Singapore's

Economic Development Board or South Korea's Economic Planning Board, or even for that of the latest NIE, Thailand's National Economic and Social Development Board, as primary agents of planning for social growth. In certain instances, the state's role has involved participation by state enterprises in fostering capital growth and development, but this arrangement appears to work only if social goals do not supplant economic profit motives or – perhaps worse – become subverted by dubious political objectives. In other cases, some form of competition occurs between private and public sectors. But the essential point is that development strategies are pragmatic and non-ideological, and include the positive encouragement of foreign direct investment.

One of the most important requirements of developmentalism is a flourishing commercial and business environment. The distinctive feature of the Pacific Asian environment is the cooperative relationship that exists between the public and the private sectors. Thus the climate in which the private sector operates is friendlier than elsewhere, contrary to what might be expected in situations where state control, through powerful bureaucracies or even militaries, is strict; conversely, the practical outlook of the public sector makes it more responsive to the needs of the private sector. This public/private sector cooperation has had a political dimension as well, resulting, for instance, in less harassment for the comprador businesses set up by the so-called 'overseas Chinese' in Southeast Asia. In the countries with more homogeneous societies, giant business conglomerates (such as the *chaebol* in South Korea) or large multipurpose trading companies (such as the *sogo shosha* in Japan) spearheaded efforts at national economic development that had the blessing of the state. In a number of cases, public agencies have gone into business as well, but this arrangement is not generally very successful unless political control over their activities is tight. Where militaries are in power, they have also ventured into business, involving themselves either indirectly through surrogates (as in Indonesia), or outright (as in Thailand).

Thus, rather than the government having no business to be in business, as is the view in the West, business in Pacific Asia is very much part of government business. As might be expected, conflicts of interest are inevitable, and often such situations spell corruption. This is not to say that Pacific Asian politics are corrupt; but certainly the notion of 'money politics' – in a grey area somewhere between corruption and political integrity – is prevalent in the region, as is amply illustrated by Japan's faction-driven electoral system. However, even where corruption does occur, it can have a formative role at certain stages of economic development; but how this should be viewed in terms of long-term societal progress and political integrity is not clear.

(3) Foreign direct investment

The role of foreign direct investment (FDI) has been crucial to Pacific Asian growth. Chapter 1 has described the webs of interdependence – both regional and global – so thoroughly that little need be added here. One aspect, however, calls for brief comment. It is interesting that, in Pacific Asia, there appears to be an absence of negative feelings about FDI – relative, say, to the situation in Latin America – which has allowed the region to make better use of the opportunities offered. This more trusting attitude may be explained, perhaps, in terms of the region's high sense of nation-building, which allowed these countries to view FDI as a concrete plank of growth. Thus, far from diminishing national sovereignty, FDI is regarded as enhancing it – a feeling that increases as the benefits are perceived, thereby, in turn, reinforcing state/regime legitimacy.

This interpretation is supported by the findings of Peter Evans in a recent study of the permeation of transnational capital in the Third World[13] – an issue to which the role of FDI is linked. Contrary to fears that had been expressed that foreign capital and transnational corporate penetration in countries whose sense of national identity was still fragile would lead to dependency and a loss of sovereignty, he came to the conclusion that the role of the state had actually been enhanced. The transnationalization, or globalization, of Asian companies appears to have had the same effect. Here again, it seems, where the sense of collective endeavour is strong, the sense of national identity suffers no damage when national, political and social divisions are ignored and new linkages formed.

(4) Deferred gratification

The phenomenon of deferred gratification is a potent and unusual feature of Pacific Asian developmentalism. The fact that workers have been willing, for example, to accept low wages in order to further the collective endeavour gives unique social meaning to the quest for national development; thus, in South Korea, the low level of workers' wages resulted not only in lower production costs but also in an attractive environment for foreign investment. In Singapore, a different approach was used, but with the same emphasis on a collective goal: a policy of high wages was pursued, but with the concomitant policy of compulsory savings through the Central Provident Fund, as well as exhortations to the public to accept Singapore's brand of limited democracy in the interests of maintaining economic competitiveness. Deferred gratification, which would seem to be more acceptable to Asian publics than to Western ones, has also led to a greater propensity to save, and this in turn has meant lower import consumption and therefore better trade balances.

Whether voluntary or not, deferred gratification must be seen as yet another sinew of the developmental state. It is particularly important in the early stages of development, since in the later stages – as Chapter 1 makes clear – domestic demand may need to be stimulated in order to stave off protectionist tendencies in external trading partners.

(5) The American security umbrella

There is no doubt that the dynamic growth of the region was made possible by the security umbrella provided by the unquestioned military superiority of the United States as part of the framework that has come to be known as the *Pax Americana*. The elements of the *Pax Americana* not only ensured US political and military hegemony (some see the United States as the Pacific's 'top dog'), but also fostered a free-trade environment in which goods from Pacific Asia found easy access to the American consumer market, and the strength of the US dollar (providing international liquidity under the Bretton Woods system) gave stability in currency exchange.

Thus, the United States both encouraged a sense of free enterprise and capitalist development and, more importantly, provided a free or open market for the importation of the region's products, notably commodities and manufactured goods. But although the United States, and (it must be hastily added) Japan, were important trading partners, it was the special character of the American politico-military umbrella that inspired the developmental mode of Pacific Asia. Now, however, as these states mature and strike a more independent posture, and perhaps in response to US efforts to correct trade imbalances, they may show signs of anti-Americanism.

The United States, for its part, may also wish to adjust its role – not only in terms of its twin budget and trade deficits and the more general problem of competitiveness, but in terms of its commitment and political will to remain in the area. But while it is possible to envisage a 'competitive coexistence', in politico-military terms, between East and West in Pacific Asia, it is more likely that the next two decades will see a period of '*Pax Americana*, Phase II' – a concept explored by Takashi Inoguchi in a recent article. This, according to Inoguchi, would imply, roughly, 'more of the same' but with 'an America which is an enlightened and experienced *primus inter pares* in an increasingly multipolar world'.[14]

DEMOCRACY AND DEVELOPMENT

The longevity of political regimes in the region has rested as much on their desire to remain in perpetual power as on the stated and perceived need of accomplishing their politico-economic goals. Because opposition was weak or suppressed, political regimes usually took the form of an overpowering single elite or a select côterie. However, as economic development proceeded, there was more opportunity for challenges to the system, and the regime itself found the need to be more open, as in South Korea and Taiwan. Even in Singapore, the need for more openness has been recognized, with a Ministry of Information being established in 1990 to initiate the two-way communication process between people and government. Nevertheless, the primacy of political power and the desire for continuity in political rule do not make for an easy transition to more competitive or adversarial politics; regime legitimacy is likely to remain intact, provided that such regimes are able to ride the crest of public demands as well as allow a greater sense of participation in decision-making, especially at the level of local government.

The relationship between those in power and those not in power and the public has rested in large part on the precondition of stability. In fact, to begin with, dissent was viewed with distaste, and, if allowed at all, tolerated only within strict limits; above all, it was not allowed to disrupt the all-important task of promoting economic growth. Whether or not a regime could deliver the goods was seen as the test of good government and regime legitimacy, and it was not regarded as particularly important that government should be subject to checks and balances. It is no accident that, as an extension of the role of elites and bureaucracies (or techno-cracies), these regimes resembled mandarinates. In the context of power and how rule is exercised in Pacific Asia, sometimes the more ruthless the elite, the more respect it commands.

If the all-important goal of national development is predicated on the creation of a capitalist class, and it has already been noted that economic development in the free-enterprise Asian Pacific political economy is likely to give rise to a middle class, then the need for strong government is also based on an ideological plane that is anti-communist. Throughout 'free' Pacific Asia, the ideology of communism, and to a lesser extent socialism, has been regarded as antagonistic to the goal and survival of the developmental state. Whereas critics took this to be no more than an excuse for reactionary behaviour, regime leaders believed in the righteousness of their cause, and in fact took the view that their strong rule provided the necessary foundation for economic modernization. In South Korea, Park Chung-hee saw his mission as one that was not only in the national interest but also benign. Under his rule, the country saw a raising of social or community consciousness that made possible sacrifices for the national good. In the *Saemaul Undong* movement, which was rural-based, social uplift was propel-led as part of an all-embracing Korean ethos that combined national pride, popular participation and pursuit of the common good.[15] In the case of Singapore, Lee Kuan Yew's efforts and the role of the People's Action Party (PAP) in a sense merged, with the result that the PAP's ideology often adjusted itself to national needs. Indeed, whereas the PAP had originally seen itself as a champion of democratic socialism, its anti-communist policies were essentially pragmatic and sometimes deviated openly from the wellspring of socialism from which it drew its inspiration; it called this approach 'socialism that works'. In Taiwan, the Kuomintang (KMT) was clearly organized along Leninist lines, but its prevail-ing ethos was very much that of a battle against the threat of communism.

This anti-communist ethos harmonized with the dictates of the cold war and the goals of a US foreign policy based on contain-ment. So long as the cause of democracy was viewed as running counter to the battle against communism (in many cases not only in the realm of ideology but also as representing the possibility of the violent overthrow of the governments in power), authoritarian regimes were tolerated, provided that they continued to furnish a bulwark against such evil forces. The support of the US administration was, in turn, regarded as a kind of legitimation of these anti-communist Pacific Asian regimes. However, as economic development has progressed and the threat of communism receded, Washington has become less supportive of undemocratic anticommunist regimes. This stance was also related to international developments that made US containment policy less viable, such as the normalization of Sino-US relations. Nevertheless, the anticommunist plank still remains in place, as evidenced by the maintenance of US ground troops in South Korea (as a deterrent to an invasion from the north), and a 'non-diplomatic' relationship with Taiwan.

CONCLUSIONS

The main themes in this chapter are that political authorities in the Pacific Asia have as their topmost priority the goal of national (economic) development, and that in fact they derive their legitimacy from their success in achieving this, within an international context that facilitates their labours. The quest for national development has led to the emergence of developmental polities with an unstated ideology of development that stresses the qualities of *strong government* and *political stability*. However, as these regimes achieve some measure of success in their development, largely based on an export-led strategy for growth, new demands arise in the system that threaten the dominant position of the political authorities in power. In South Korea, 'military strongman rule' appears no longer to be acceptable, so that some form of political contestation based on political parties seems to be inevitable. In Singapore, although the PAP continues to hold power, its rule can no longer be as absolute or overriding as before. In Taiwan, the hegemony of the KMT has been continuously assailed in the past few years.

What, then, is the outlook for the future? Robert Scalapino has observed that three basic types of political system have evolved in Pacific Asia: the Leninist system, the authoritarian-pluralist system and the parliamentary-democratic system.[16] In terms of our construct of the developmental state, the countries that have achieved the greatest growth have been largely of the second category. Japan could be said to fall into the third category, but its political style is more characteristic of the second, and certainly its regime approach is to steer the economy to great heights. The challenges of the 1990s, according to Professor Scalapino, will revolve around openness versus stability (whether to be more or to be less democratic), nation-building (the reconciling of religious and ethnic demands with nation-state survival) and political institutionalization (whether 'men' or processes are more important).[17] Among the various issues that are likely to arise, the political bases of economic development will surely present the greatest challenge.

This in turn will revolve around the role of the state in development, and what policies may be appropriate in the rapidly changing circumstances of political evolution, economic interdependence and technological progress. For example, will earlier strategies, such as export-led growth, provide for sustained development in the future? There are signs that this emphasis is already being modified; but how will such shifts be implemented? If, paradoxically, the state is still strong but not institutionalized, the role of elites will become crucial.

In this respect, it is worth recalling that developmental polities are usually presided over by *strong personalities*, who leave in their path an imprint that is difficult to disregard. However, it is apparent that such forms of 'personal rule' are less acceptable to mass publics in these societies as economic development proceeds. Their roles are still critical, though, and it should be recognized that in Pacific Asia personalities are important symbols of political power. Asian political publics might continue to find it hard to oppose those who are in power, but they may well learn to renounce such leaders once they are out of power if their stay has been 'short' (the striking example here being that of South Korea's Chun Doo Hwan). On the other hand, there is a reverence for a leader like Lee Kuan Yew and at least little stated disrespect for the late Generalissimo Chiang Kaishek.

The challenge for these systems is how their political regimes will make the transition to circumstances in which a good part of the goal of national development has been achieved – a stage of development indicated by the rising political awareness of the more affluent segment of society and a recognition that some form of contestation for political power should be allowed. Politics can be expected to become more pluralistic but not in the democratic mode of the West.[18] Indeed, it can be argued that political competition is not a process that is well understood either in theory or in practice in Pacific Asia, since it is regarded as leading to violence, not accommodation. Even in Japan, democracy exists only in modified form, in that the ruling party is assured of almost perpetual power.

The dilemma, of course, is that continued economic growth as a function of the developmental polity may not be so assured if the basis of politics is altered – and altered it must be as a result of political maturation arising from improved economic and social conditions. The high-flyers of Pacific Asia are, in a sense, the prisoners of their own success; for, once developmentalism is accepted as the basis of state survival, it is a race in which one has to continue to participate in order to prosper. For the 1990s, much will depend on the international environment, both in economic and in security terms.

Chapter 4

The newly industrializing economies

The most dramatic growth rates in the region, during the past few years, have been recorded by Pacific Asia's four newly industrializing economies (NIEs): South Korea, Taiwan, Hong Kong and Singapore. This chapter will examine the specific ways in which each of these four countries has approached some of the issues raised in the preceding chapters.

From 1986 to 1988 South Korea figured as the world's fastest-growing economy, with a growth rate of around 12 per cent for three consecutive years. Singapore recovered from a severe setback in 1985 to record a 11 per cent growth figure in 1988. Hong Kong and Taiwan both recorded nearly 7 per cent. The share of total world trade held by the four NIEs had grown from 2 per cent in the mid-1960s to 10 per cent by 1989. Their share of world exports of manufactured goods reached 11 per cent in 1987 – just short of Japan. In several respects these four high-flyers seem close to graduation from the class of NIEs.

Adulthood, however, brings new challenges with it. As the international trading environment becomes more complicated, all four face a challenge to their traditional dependence on export-fuelled growth. Rising protectionist feeling in their key markets – all four send at least 25 per cent of their exports to the United States – is supplemented by growing competition from less developed countries in certain important labour-intensive industrial sectors. Although their responses are not identical, they have all begun to take this danger into account.

A further challenge is presented by pressures for democratization. As Chapter 3 makes so clear, the early stages of economic growth are closely related to political stability. In the Pacific Asian NIEs this has not always been combined with an open or broadly based democratic process. Now, however, continued economic growth has created a professional and entrepreneurial middle class which, while on the one hand favouring stability and only gradual change, is, on the other hand, beginning to call for a voice in the political process to match the economic benefits received. Therefore, just as the four NIEs are being forced to grapple with the benefits – and costs – of their own economic progress, so they are also facing crucial issues of political succession and openness in their political systems. Once again, as in their responses to economic challenge, their reactions have varied.

ECONOMIC STRATEGIES OF THE NIEs

Export-led growth, through making the best use of comparative advantage, has become the hallmark of the four Asian NIEs.[1] Hong Kong has always been outward-oriented, but it was not until the 1960s that the other three began to give priority to export-oriented strategies based on manufactured goods. They concentrated first on light, labour-intensive industries, following this by a move, in South Korea, Singapore and Taiwan (but not Hong Kong), into certain heavy industries, though often with mixed results.

There is no doubt that for all four NIEs political survival was closely tied to economic development. It is a curious fact that all four are geographically and politically isolated: they could thus count on popular support in the struggle to survive as entities. Singapore is a predominantly Chinese city-state floating in a sea of Malays. Hong Kong, to use Richard Hughes's memorable expression, is a 'borrowed place on borrowed time', always aware of the weight of China so close at hand. Taiwan, itself claiming to rule all China, is ever conscious of the 'threat' from the mainland. South Korea, another part-country, has never felt any real affinity with its erratic northern neighbour. Whether or not the nearby external 'threat' was perceived as real, it seems to have engendered a sense of competition and a consensus that development was essential.

The role of government remains a controversial factor, but in at least three of the NIEs concrete economic performance became the touchstone of political legitimacy and national progress. Hong Kong has often been described as a classic laissez-faire economy, but in reality there has been a limited degree of governmental direction, to create what is aptly labelled as 'positive non-interventionism'; the government acts as a facilitator. In the other three NIEs, however, governmental intervention has been far more overt. Not only through a commitment to development planning but also through close relations with industry, successive governments have endeavoured to 'pick winners' in industrial sectors. Costly mistakes were made in both South Korea and Singapore in the 1970s, but the administrative and technocratic elites had an impressive record in designing economic policies through into the 1980s. Now, however, these governments are anxious to take a lower profile. Indeed, under 'democratization', both South Korea and Taiwan are more subject to pressures from domestic parties and interest groups. Ironically, Hong Kong, fearful of slipping technologically behind its three rivals, is beginning to show slightly more governmental direction of industry.

All four NIEs are densely populated and poorly endowed with natural resources. As a result, they have to rely not only on imported raw materials but also on making the best use of their human resources. Both South Korea and Taiwan have put particular emphasis on basic education, which has given them efficient and well-qualified labour forces.

Japan has acted both as a model and as a mentor to the four NIEs – to a greater extent than nationals of those countries might wish to admit but less than outside observers believe. Japan is either the first or the second largest source both of imports and of investment for all the NIEs. It has become, to put it in oversimplified terms, the main supplier to the NIEs of intermediate components for consumer and communication products destined for the United States. Its economic aid to the NIEs has decreased to a minimal level, but technology transfer has helped to compensate in part. Japan, despite its continuing trade surpluses with the NIEs, has in recent years taken a more sympathetic line than other OECD countries towards the NIEs' own trade surpluses with the OECD; the NIEs, however, tend to regard Japan with some ambivalence.

SOUTH KOREA

The September 1988 Seoul Olympics not only brought South Korea immense economic and diplomatic benefits, but symbolized the country's aspirations for greater prominence on the international stage. South Korea is, however, going through a difficult transitional period, as it reaps the benefits but also suffers the pains of being both a newly industrializing and a newly democratizing country. President Roh Tae-woo, therefore, finds himself forced not only to answer more effectively the calls for further political liberalization and economic restructuring, but also to find a new unifying 'vision' for his people.

South Korea is a near-perfect example of the 'developmental state'. The economic devastation left by the 1950–3 war, together with the constant threat to security from the North, called for strong government, strong personal leadership, and a collective commitment to economic growth and nation-building. This is precisely what South Korea got: an authoritarian-bureaucratic style of government, with the military playing a strong role; and a leader, President Park Chung-hee, whose skilful mobilization of the energies of the people produced the economic miracle of the 1960s and 1970s. The structures created at that time – the powerful conglomerates, or *chaebol* (the epitome of a fruitful public/private sector relationship), vigorously supported by an *over* powerful bureaucracy/technocracy – are essentially still in place.

But in the meantime South Korean society has been changing. Power has been diffused. The *chaebol*, which effectively dominate South Korean business, have become less dependent on the government; a well-educated middle class has sprung into being; resentment at the role of the military in politics has grown; and, finally, the workers, once willing to accept low wages in the interests of economic growth, are prepared to 'defer gratification' no longer. In 1987 the government of President Chun Doo Hwan was forced to take seriously demands not only for a fairer distribution of the benefits of economic development, but also for a greater share of the political cake, when many middle-class Koreans began to join in the anti-government demonstrations. The nationwide character and the broader social involvement of these protests forced Roh (nominated as the presidential candidate of the ruling Democratic Justice Party – DJP), and ultimately Chun, to realize that political change had to take place. Aware that martial law would have caused bloodshed and chaos, and almost certainly would have meant Seoul's loss of the 1988 Olympics, which meant so much to all Koreans, Roh put together a 'democratization package' that met almost all of the opposition's demands, including direct presidential elections.

The December 1987 elections aroused popular interest to an unprecedented degree, but this was not translated into radical political change. In the National Assembly elections of April 1988, DJP complacency and self-inflicted wounds, combined with opposition enthusiasm and strong regional voting biases, led to the DJP failing to secure an overall majority over the combined opposition – the first time ever that a government had failed to win a parliamentary majority.[2]

The most significant political change under the Roh government, however, came with the behind-the-scenes negotiating that produced the new Democratic Liberal Party in February 1990.[3] The DLP, formed from an alliance of the DJP with two out of the three main opposition parties, became the majority party. Roh clearly gained most, while the gamble was the greatest for Kim Young-sam, a long-time opposition leader. The intention had been to emulate the Japanese Liberal Democratic Party in creating stable and effectively one-party politics, but power-bargaining and factional manoeuvring have remained a constant factor, and the possibility of disintegration still exists.

The formation of the DLP coincided with a vigorous debate within South Korea about the direction of the economy, as many Koreans became convinced that the drop from double-digit growth in the mid-1980s to 6.5 per cent in 1989 constituted an economic 'crisis'. Called into question were some of the basic economic policies of the late 1980s. Earlier, in the first half of the 1980s, economic planners had called for a 'changing role' for the government towards private economic activities (i.e., in theory, to be less interventionist). Exports were to remain the leading edge of growth, but the domestic market would be more exposed to foreign competition, including inward FDI. Reforms were attempted in three areas – import liberalization, industrial policy realignment and financial liberalization – and these were given even greater emphasis by the early Roh cabinets. However, there has been considerable opposition both within and outside the government to some of the liberalization proposals, and this has slowed progress.[4]

The boom growth years of 1986–8 came on the back of a number of external changes – the 'three lows' – which, on balance, favoured the South Korean economy. First, the Korean won appreciated slightly against the US dollar and significantly depreciated against the yen, thereby encouraging Korean exports, particularly to the United States. Second, with much of the Korean foreign debt pegged to US prime and Euromarket rates, the decline in international interest rates assisted repayments. And, third, the falling oil prices enabled substantial savings on energy import costs. As a result, South Korea was able in 1986 to record its first-ever joint trade and current-account surplus, and the first reduction in its total debt, which was further reduced to $32 billion by the end of 1988, from a peak of $47 billion in 1985.

In 1989, however, both trade and current-account surpluses shrank owing to a loss in export competitiveness, caused by the delayed impact of the continued and accelerating appreciation of the won against the US dollar during 1987–8 and dramatic wage rises (averaging around 20 per cent in the manufacturing sector in both 1988 and 1989). Since 1987 there has been a marked increase in labour–management disputes, as workers have tried to redress past inequities.[5]

South Korea has been making a conscious effort to diversify its trading partners and to wean itself away from overdependence on Japan and the United States. The situation is complicated by the fact that its trade deficit with Japan (which peaked at around $5 billion in both 1986 and 1987) and trade surplus with the United States (which stood at around $9 billion for both 1987 and 1988) tend all too easily to become politicized.

South Korea's trading activities have given it strong links both with OECD countries (a factor that is likely to swing the balance of voting in favour of South Korea being admitted to OECD membership in the early 1990s) and with the Middle East oil producers. For the other Asian countries, South Korea can be an important source of intermediate goods, and of the technology necessary for modernization, at prices competitive with the Japanese; Korean manufacturing FDI in Southeast Asia in 1988 equalled the combined total of the preceding fifteen years. In 1987 South Korea actually inaugurated its own External Economic Cooperation Fund, aimed at giving assistance to industrial projects in developing Asian nations.

Until recently, South Korea's economic success has owed a lot to its sense of competition with North Korea. Now, however, in the economic sphere at least, South Korea displays a nationalistic self-confidence in its dealings with the North. This led President Roh to talk in 1988 of a kind of 'big brother' policy, implying that increasing economic disadvantage would force North Korea to abandon its ominous and often erratic policies towards the South.

In the South, the changes in Eastern Europe in 1989–90, in particular the rapid moves towards unification on the part of the two Germanies, revived the popular mood for reunification and raised hopes of change in North Korea. Renewed manoeuvring between the two sides in the summer of 1990 led to an unprecedented meeting between the two prime ministers in September, followed by further meetings in October and December. However, mutual suspicion persists, precluding any real breakthrough in contacts.

The United States has been the most important partner for South Korea. The US–South Korean relationship has been a deeply asymmetrical one, but of late South Korea has exhibited the desire, and ability, to act more independently. In recent years the main source of tension between the two countries has come from trade issues. Echoing earlier 'Japan-bashing', US interest groups and politicians have called for protectionist measures against South Korean exports, for greater opening of the South Korean market, for adherence to international copyright and patent conventions, and, most recently, for currency realignment.[6] The United States used the threat of punitive action under the notorious 'Super 301' clause of the 1988 Omnibus Trade Act to extract further concessions in both 1989 and 1990. As a result, anti-Americanism, always latent in Korean society, has been revived, and younger Koreans, resentful of US political support for authoritarian government, are now reinforcing the hostility of trade groups hit by US pressure. The presence and role of the US forces in South Korea has also become controversial; domestic political and budgetary pressures in both countries are forcing the two governments into reorganizing the military command structures and, in stages, carrying out the partial withdrawal of US forces (in early 1990 the United States proposed withdrawing 5,000 troops by 1993).[7]

South Korea's other 'special relationship' – with Japan – has been even more complex and chequered. The exchange of prime ministerial and presidential visits that has taken place since 1983 has done much to improve relations, at least at the governmental level; but, as was shown by the controversies surrounding the Emperor's apology and the Japanese treatment of Korean residents during Roh's visit to Japan in May 1990, the emotional tension between the two peoples is never far below the surface.

Since the early 1970s South Korea has maintained a policy of establishing contacts with all countries regardless of ideology, but this policy acquired a new dimension in 1983, when a *nordpolitik* to normalize relations with China and the Soviet Union was announced. Little real progress was made, so Roh has tried to hasten the process. He had some notable successes, with several East European countries establishing trade offices in Seoul, before Hungary took the lead in giving full diplomatic recognition in February 1989. The disintegration of the communist bloc in Eastern Europe led to a series of diplomatic recognitions: by Poland in November, Yugoslavia in December 1989, and Czechoslovakia, Bulgaria and Mongolia in March 1990. But it was China that Roh was really angling for – primarily in order to obtain political recognition, but also to get China to restrain North Korea from adventurist military action and to establish a major trading relationship. However, although the current Chinese leadership is in favour of developing economic contacts with the South (trade in 1989 was estimated at $3.1 billion), its ideological bent and continued close relationship with the North are likely to postpone political recognition.[8]

In contrast, relations with the Soviet Union have moved ahead fast. Trade, sports and cultural exchanges have increased greatly since Soviet participation in the Seoul Oympics in 1988. In December 1989, the Soviet Union agreed to establish consular relations; Kim Young-sam, now in his DLP representative role, visited Moscow in March 1990 (when he talked with Gorbachev); and, in June 1990, Roh himself met Gorbachev in a historic meeting in San Francisco.[9] Official relations were established in September 1990, and Roh visited Moscow in December 1990.

South Korea remains something of an anomaly in international relations. There are signs that the situation is gradually improving – Roh's address to the United Nations in October 1988 (the first ever by a Korean head of state) was one such sign, the award of 'sectoral dialogue partner' status by the ASEAN leaders in July 1989 was another – but the Koreans are still living with the stigma of being a half-country, not completely reconciled with themselves. East Germany's moves towards unification with the Federal Republic in 1990 were undertaken in close collaboration with the West and with the understanding of the Soviet Union; the Koreas, North and South alike, have no such protective environment. In his inaugural speech in February 1988, President Roh spoke for all his people when he expressed the hope that Korea, 'once a peripheral country in East Asia', would take 'a central position in the international community'.[10] This, surely, is the new unifying 'vision' that must carry the country forward to the next phase of development.

TAIWAN

Taiwan's recent economic – and, indeed, political – development is very similar in many respects to that of South Korea. Following a decade of solid growth averaging around 9 per cent per annum, it recorded double-digit growth in both 1986 and 1987, and in February 1988 its foreign-exchange reserves reached a peak of US $76 billion (second only to Japan). In 1987 the overall trade surplus peaked at $20 billion, of which $16 billion was with the United States. As with South Korea, Taiwan's economic success has brought costs as well as benefits. The growing need for economic restructuring has been accompanied by rising pressures for a reorganization of the outdated political institutions. In 1986, not uninfluenced by events in the Philippines and South Korea, President Chiang Ching-kuo began to set in motion a programme of 'reform from above', which his successor Lee Teng-hui has built on. Nevertheless, political reform is still a cautious, step-by-step process designed to prevent either a conservative backlash or runaway liberalization.

Taiwan's pattern of economic development has differed from that of South Korea in two significant respects. First, there is a much greater reliance on foreign direct investment (FDI), so that, for example, between 1973 and 1980 FDI accounted for approximately 50 per cent of total investment in the electronics sector. (Taiwan's external borrowing has been negligible.) Second, small and medium-sized enterprises play a more important role in the economy (enterprises employing fewer than 50 people still contribute 94 per cent of Taiwan's total production of goods and services). These smaller units of production, though based on the indigenous structure of Chinese/Taiwanese business, were encouraged by the Taiwanese government in a deliberate attempt to prevent alternative power-centres, such as the *chaebol* in South Korea, from emerging. This difference in the development strategies of the two countries relates to differences in their political power-bases. In Taiwan, where 3 million mainlanders, holding political power, regulate the economic activities of 10 million Taiwanese, the government could not risk upsetting its power-base; the Korean government, whose power-base is more secure, had no such need to diffuse the units of production. The smaller companies that characterize Taiwan have the advantage of being able to respond flexibly to changing world demand in light manufactured goods, but they are handicapped when it comes to developing high technology, which calls for large R&D expenditure.

Taiwan's emphasis on an export strategy based on light manufactured goods, adopted in the mid-1960s, had already been altered to some extent by the cumulative effect of the two oil shocks of the 1970s. Since the early 1980s a pronounced shift towards high technology and skill-intensive activities has taken place, three sectors – information, electronics and machinery – being designated 'strategic industries'. The government established the Hsinchu Science-based Industrial Park in 1979 and has encouraged, through incentives, technology inputs from abroad.[11] It has also tried gradually to reduce its own direct ownership of enterprises, and in May 1989 the cabinet approved plans for privatizing or partially privatizing fifteen major banks and industrial corporations. In short, the government's economic planning agencies, under President Lee, are trying to aid industrial restructuring by moving towards a coordinating role, rather than following the directive, at times autocratic, style that prevailed previously.

Although import restrictions have been considerably relaxed since the early 1980s, Taiwanese officials have fought a tough rearguard action against external pressure for market-opening, primarily from the United States. As in South Korea – and, indeed, Japan – the agricultural sector has been a particularly difficult and sensitive one for the Americans to open up (as the May 1988 anti-American demonstrations showed). Taiwan was also initially reluctant to revalue its currency as a way of reducing its trade surplus with the United States, but between the September 1985 G-5 Plaza meeting and April 1988 the New Taiwan dollar did appreciate by 41 per cent against the US dollar (the sharpest revaluation for any of the four NIEs). Taiwan's low-cost, labour-intensive industries, such as clothing, toys and footwear, have suffered most, but the appreciation has encouraged the shift to higher-technology products. Taiwan is now beginning to suffer a labour shortage, and in early 1990 the government allowed companies, particularly those involved in fourteen designated major infrastructural projects, to bring in labourers from elsewhere in Pacific Asia.

Not only changing the composition of its exports but also diversifying its trading partners, has become a priority for Taiwan; for, like South Korea, it depends heavily on the United States as a market (still 44 per cent of total exports in 1987) and Japan as a source of imports (34 per cent of total imports). Already in February 1988, as a first step, the government had announced a five-year market diversification and import expansion plan. The EC has been a clear target, but so, for the first time, are socialist-bloc countries. A large Taiwanese trade delegation visited the Soviet Union in October 1988, and trade with the East European countries is steadily increasing. Hoping no doubt to emulate the South Korean experience, Taiwan scored its first diplomatic breakthrough with the establishment of a trade office in Hungary in 1990.

But the greatest interest lies in China. President Lee, a native Taiwanese, has toned down the old rhetoric about 'recovering' China and, in practice, has moved to redefine policy towards the mainland. There has been a gradual modification of the traditional policy of the 'three no's' (no contact, no negotiations and no compromise), although the events of April–June 1989 in China have slowed the pace of rapprochement. In July 1988, following on President Chiang's decision in November 1987 to allow Taiwanese to visit relatives on the mainland, the Thirteenth Congress of the ruling Kuomintang (KMT) party adopted a number of measures to encourage sports and cultural exchanges and to ease indirect trade. During 1989 over half a million Taiwanese visited China, and in April 1989, for the first time ever, a cabinet minister actually visited Beijing to attend a conference of the Asian Development Bank (ADB). In the spring of 1990 the government relaxed restrictions on trips to China made by businessmen and parliamentarians, and on certain imports from China. China–Taiwan indirect trade – through Hong Kong and Singapore – rose from around $1.5 billion in 1987 to an estimated $3.5 billion in 1989, thereby making China Taiwan's fifth largest trading partner. Although technically prohibited by the Taiwanese government, investment in China soared, with, according to some estimates, over $1 billion invested in joint ventures, two-thirds of this in Fujian province, by the end of 1989. In his inaugural address in May 1990, President Lee argued for setting up 'channels of communication' with China, so signalling a desire to end the 'three no's' policy.

Since early 1989 senior Taiwanese leaders began to float the idea of a 'one China, two governments' formula as an alternative to China's 'one country, two systems' approach.[12] Ironically, the Chinese leadership, which had welcomed the more relaxed attitude of the Taiwanese government over economic contacts since 1987, has been critical of these new formulations. It is clearly concerned about the pace and direction of political reform under Lee and the isolated, if increasingly articulate, demands for Taiwan's independence coming from opposition groups. Generational change and social pluralism are gradually chipping away at loyalty towards the idea of a much larger China, incorporating the mainland; indeed, for the younger generation reunification has become an abstract idea.[13]

President Lee, like President Chiang in his later years, has realized that the leadership has become out of touch with the aspirations not just of students, but also of the growing middle class, for a more representative form of government and a better quality of life (issues of social welfare and pollution control are being increasingly voiced). However, the present constitutional order, with the three chambers of the parliament heavily dominated by members who were elected in 1947 and have not faced re-election since, can be altered only gradually, not least because structural revision raises questions about the legitimacy of the KMT's claim to represent the whole of China.

The newly legalized main opposition party, the Democratic Progressive Party (DPP), is becoming more active both inside and outside parliament. It certainly made notable gains in the elections of December 1989, both at the local level and at that of the Legislative Council (Yuan), even if the KMT remained predominant. But it is weakened by factional in-fighting, as well as a shortage of talent and financial resources, and its precise position is hard to determine. Eleven DPP members of the National Assembly were actually suspended in March 1990 for swearing an oath of loyalty to the 'people of Taiwan' rather than to the 'Republic of China'.[14]

Inevitably, growing public pressure for a reassessment of fundamental policies is having repercussions on Taiwan's perception of itself in relation not only to China but to its isolated diplomatic position in general. President Lee has adopted a more 'flexible diplomacy', which plays down the old policy of not dealing with those countries that recognized China, and there are beginning to be signs that the country's diplomatic isolation may be lessening. In 1989 four African and Caribbean states recognized Taiwan, and, when Lee himself visited Singapore in March 1990, he agreed to be described as the 'President of Taiwan'. Saudi Arabia's recognition of China in July 1990 was a blow, but Taiwan is likely to find continued diplomatic gains elsewhere in the poorer Third World.

Attempts to gain – or regain – positions in multilateral economic organizations such as the IMF or GATT still hinge, of course, on the question of China's membership. When China joined the ADB in 1986, Taiwan, though disgruntled, did remain a member. Since June 1989 and the events in Tiananmen Square, China, for its part, has become even more nervous and rigid about Taiwan's position in the world, and hence more rigid than ever towards Taiwan. However, with China's own international standing badly shaken, Taiwan is actually much more likely to be treated as a separate 'entity' by the global community. Its political emergence onto the world stage will be even more complicated than South Korea's, but the 1990s will certainly see a gradual extension of its room for manoeuvre in foreign affairs.

HONG KONG

The evolving China–Taiwan relationship is deeply affected by the nature of China's relationship with another NIE, Hong Kong – not least because Chinese leaders are viewing the new administrative and economic structure for the Special Administrative Region (SAR) of Hong Kong, as it will become after July 1997, as a model for the future incorporation of Taiwan.

As regards trading patterns, Hong Kong shares with Singapore an outward-looking economy with a very small domestic market. Manufacturing industry has always made an important contribution to growth and, traditionally, has been heavily concentrated in the production of light consumer goods, such as textiles and clothing, electrical goods, and plastics. However, since the end of the 1970s, increased competition in overseas markets, more stringent quota restrictions on textiles and garments, and rising labour costs have led to increasing moves upmarket. But Hong Kong remains the world's largest exporter of clothing because it is able to source low-cost labour in China for its labour-intensive activities in clothing manufacture and has encouraged high-fashion and high-value-added operations within Hong Kong. In the electronics industry, the Hong Kong government has sought not only to encourage opportunities for technology transfer by means of foreign investment (by the end of 1984 nearly 40 per cent of all FDI was in this sector), but also to raise the level of local technological awareness and indigenous R&D activity. Further technological development, however, is hampered by the past failure of government to encourage enough technocrats and the current 'brain drain' of skilled young people going abroad.

Although uncertainty about the future Chinese role in Hong Kong in the aftermath of the 1984 Sino-British agreement and the world-wide economic recession contributed to a virtually zero-growth figure for 1985, Hong Kong's return to double-digit growth in 1986 and 1987 actually owed much to a new economic relationship with China. The changes in China's own economic policies during the 1980s, and the efforts applied to developing the neighbouring Shenzhen Special Economic Zone (SEZ) and Guangdong province, led to a revival of Hong Kong's traditional role as an entrepôt, a trans-shipment centre and a gateway for the China trade. China is now Hong Kong's largest trading partner and the third largest investor in its manufacturing sector, while Hong Kong is China's largest export market. Since 1984, Hong Kong-based manufacturers have been investing heavily in China, providing around 65 per cent of China's stock of FDI by the end of 1987. Estimates in mid-1988 suggest that the number of workers directly employed in manufacturing in south China by Hong Kong companies was larger than that for Hong Kong's own workforce in the manufacturing sector.[15]

Although the ever-closer linkage of the two economies – or, to be more precise, the Guangdong and Hong Kong economies – has benefited Hong Kong,[16] it does make it more difficult for Hong Kong to insulate itself from the vagaries of the Chinese economy, whether China's high inflation in mid-1988 (which affected Hong Kong's imported foodstuffs) or the changes in Chinese foreign economic policy enforced after the June 1989 incidents. The Hong Kong economy was already decelerating in 1988, when GDP growth dropped to 7 per cent, but the mid-1989 events in China, combined with the attendant uncertainties of the future Hong Kong/China relationship, led to growth dropping right down to 2.5 per cent in 1989, and projections of only 3 per cent for 1990. Hong Kong has also put emphasis in recent years on its expanding role as a financial services centre – a role which, despite the traumatic local effects of the October 1987 stock-market crash, is likely to continue. Hong Kong now ranks sixth among the world's foreign-exchange markets, for example. The whole securities system was reviewed in early 1988 to provide for a more balanced and better-regulated development of the financial sector in future. A role for Hong Kong as the regional financial centre for south China seems assured, but it is less certain that it can provide all of China's national financial needs after 1997.

The British and Hong Kong authorities are well aware that increased affluence has brought demands not only for better public and social services but also for more representative government. The Sino-British Joint Declaration of September 1984, achieved after two years of convoluted negotiations, had set out principles for the administration of the Hong Kong SAR, which would be given a 'high degree of autonomy' and would be allowed to maintain its 'previous capitalist system and life-style . . . unchanged for 50 years'. Since then, a Sino-British Joint Liaison Group has been meeting regularly to discuss administrative arrangements in detail. The British have regarded these sessions as having an educative element, as being a means of preparing the communist Chinese for the task of governing a complex capitalist enclave.

However, the events in China of mid-1989 totally changed the context of discussions about democracy and autonomy for Hong Kong. The Chinese student demonstrations and their violent suppression in June 1989 highlighted the dilemmas and difficulties that Hong Kong and its people face. During successive weekends in May and June of that year more than a million Hong Kong people marched for democracy and freedom in China. Until then the Hong Kong people's confidence in their future prosperity had been largely based on the Chinese leadership's apparent commitment to modernize China. The June massacres shattered trust, at one blow, in the Chinese leadership, the Sino-British Joint Declaration and the draft Basic Law, the second draft of which had been made public in February 1989. The political apathy characteristic of the Hong Kong population disappeared and the hitherto small democracy movement received a major boost.[17]

Neither Britain nor China is prepared to contemplate renegotiating the Joint Declaration. The Chinese have been keen to press on with formulation of the Basic Law, while simply issuing statements that have done little to calm the people of Hong Kong. The

British government lays the onus on China to allay the fears of the Hong Kong people; they, however, look to the British government to reassure them in the only two ways still open: greater democracy within the colony and an 'insurance policy' deriving from the right of abode elsewhere after 1997.

The British government has been excessively cautious on the question of pre-1997 political reform and the introduction of an elected element into the Legislative Council (Legco). Senior Chinese officials, including Deng Xiaoping himself, expressed firm opposition to universal suffrage in Hong Kong,[18] and, while the Hong Kong government knows through its own survey results that a substantial majority is in favour of direct elections, it has been reluctant to force the pace of electoral reform beyond that allowed by China. The final draft of the Basic Law, approved by the National People's Congress in April 1990, showed only marginal evidence of Chinese concessions to Hong Kong sensitivities.[19] It allows for only 20 out of 60 Legco seats to be directly elected in 1997, and 30 in 2003 (a considerably more restricted programme than even the conservative Legco members expected). Nevertheless, at least the Hong Kong authorities will be holding direct elections for their one-third share of Legco in September 1991, the first such elections, and embryonic political parties are beginning to flourish.

Out of Hong Kong's present population of 5.7 million, 3.2 million people hold British 'dependent territory' passports; yet, apart from those few who have acquired full British citizenship with right of abode (for example, by residing in the United Kingdom for some years), all these people will become Chinese nationals after 1997. Hong Kong is already suffering from emigration to other English-speaking countries (net outflow in 1989 was 42,000), and this flow is expected to increase during the 1990s; crucially, it is professionals and skilled workers, on whom the future of Hong Kong depends, who form the bulk of those leaving. The British government has been able to do little to reassure Hong Kong opinion, partly because questions of nationality, right of abode and passports have become highly charged domestically. In view of the open opposition of Conservative right-wingers (and the Labour Party) to the spring 1990 legislation offering nationality to 50,000 families, it will find it difficult to go beyond this limited offer.[20]

Hong Kong's international legal status after 1997 is also under active consideration, as was shown by its admission to the GATT in 1986. Its participation, in its own right, in a number of international and regional organizations seems certain, but that representation has to be made in such a way as not to compromise China's sovereignty over Hong Kong. A separate role for Hong Kong in such organizations as the GATT, the IMF and the ADB will be one way of reassuring nervous business circles about the future stability and prosperity of Hong Kong.

SINGAPORE

During its period of British colonial rule, Singapore operated as a centre for entrepôt trade, and, apart from a brief flirtation with an import-substitution strategy immediately following independence, it has maintained its role as a city open to the outside world and as a commercial centre for Southeast Asia (thereby playing a pivotal trade and financial role in the development of its less-advanced ASEAN neighbours). Like Hong Kong, it has acted as a conduit for the China trade. Singapore has developed a worker-welfare state, in which the education, trade-union and savings systems have played key roles; but this pressure-cooker atmosphere, while having clear economic merits, has hardly been designed to produce conciliatory and participatory politics or a relaxed society.

Prime Minister Lee Kuan Yew has vigorously pursued a policy of attracting foreign capital to promote industrialization, so that by 1985 foreign multinationals accounted for 70 per cent of manufactured output and 82 per cent of exports. The policy of promoting labour-intensive manufacturing, however, began to suffer from labour shortages in the late 1970s and so, in 1979, the government decided to upgrade the country's industrial structure. By sharply raising wages, which previously had been kept deliberately low, and shifting the emphasis to high-value-added industries (such as computers, electronics and machinery) as well as downstream petrochemical activities to complement the existing oil-refining sector, the government tried to do too much too quickly. Global economic recession (particularly affecting the oil-refining and ship-repair industries), a general decline in international competitiveness as a result of rising business costs, and adaptation problems of the low-value, labour-intensive companies combined to shake the Singaporean economy to the extent that negative GNP growth (−1.8 per cent) was recorded in 1985 for the first time.

The government promptly established an Economic Committee, headed by Brigadier-General Lee Hsien Loong, son of the prime minister, to review policy. In the short run, employers' savings burdens were eased, corporate taxes were reduced, wages were frozen. For the medium term, further efforts to create an infrastructure of qualified personnel and R&D activity were recommended. These prompt adjustments, assisted by more favourable external factors such as the appreciation of the yen, helped Singapore rapidly to regain international competitiveness and restore growth.

There was a fresh inflow of foreign capital in the late 1980s; FDI into Singapore in 1987 increased by 22 per cent over the preceding year. Japanese companies were the largest investors in 1987, although the United States still remains the largest investor in terms of cumulative investment. Both countries have actively invested in manufacturing industries, particularly in electronic components, computer peripherals and electrical products. The electronics industry has been the key to Singapore's recovery, since it now provides 40 per cent of all Singaporean domestic exports, and has replaced oil-refining as Singapore's top industry. However, because of fears that shortages of skilled labour would hamper further development, the government liberalized its immigration rules in mid-1989 (Hong Kong residents were to be given special priority).

The main international services (transport and communications, financial and business services) have also grown steadily in importance, so that together they represented about one-third of GDP by the mid-1980s. With a gradual transfer of labour-intensive production facilities to Malaysia, Singapore will continue to develop as a service centre for Southeast Asia. Since its stock market is still tiny by comparison with those of Japan or Hong Kong, it is anxious to develop primarily as a centre for fund-management. Furthermore, following financial deregulation among the ASEAN countries, Singapore will become a major source of ASEAN offshore banking. Finally, since 1986 Singapore has been the world's top port in terms of shipping tonnage. Tourist arrivals started to rise again (with the Japanese in the van) in the late 1980s after several years of disappointing growth.

In fact, its invisible earnings, together with net capital inflows, help to offset the trade deficits that Singapore continues to run, so that small current-account surpluses can be achieved. In the second half of the 1980s, its trade deficits have slowly grown from US $3 billion in 1986 to over $5 billion in 1989. Like its fellow Asian NIEs, it is heavily dependent on the United States as an export market (23 per cent of exports in 1989) and Japan as a source of imports (21 per cent in 1989). However, although Singapore does suffer from a trade deficit with Japan (of about the same level as that of Taiwan), it is the only Asian NIE, recently, actually to have been in deficit with the United States as well, at least until 1986. Singapore has been aided in its recovery since 1986 by the improved performance of at least two of its ASEAN trading partners, Thailand and Malaysia, although the proportion of intra-ASEAN trade in its overall trade continues to decline slowly. Since mid-1990 Singapore has begun to promote the concept of a 'growth triangle' with neighbouring Johore state in Malaysia and Batam island in Indonesia, but there is some suspicion that the lion's share of the benefits of closer integration would flow to Singapore.

Although the Singapore government has on the whole avoided taking a *dirigiste* attitude to foreign trade, it has influenced the direction of domestic and foreign investments into industries it deems vital to economic development. Like Taiwan, Singapore set up state-owned companies (still over 600 in 1986) to establish an industrial presence in those sectors in which private enterprise was unwilling or unable to take the risk. However, one of the longer-term recommendations of the 1985 Economic Committee was for less government intervention and more privatization; moves are being made in this direction, but the pace is slow. Moreover, the past domination of industry by public-sector companies and foreign multinationals has left Singapore, by comparison with the other NIEs, with a society that is short on risk-taking, entrepreneurial skills.

If government over-regulation and popular aversion to risk-taking seem to characterize the economic system, this is even more true of the political system. Lee Kuan Yew's People's Action Party (PAP) has maintained an overwhelming majority in the parliament ever since Singapore became internally self-governing in 1959. Prime Minister Lee has led the PAP – and the country – with a strong grip, despite the emergence of a succession of younger leaders who have competed to become heir-apparent. During the late 1980s, Lee several times toyed with the idea of retiring from the premiership, but stayed on: despite the overwhelming mandate received by the PAP in the September 1988 election (80 out of 81 seats), he has shown little faith in the ability of others to lead the party effectively.[21] In November 1990, however, he finally handed over to his deputy, Goh Chok Tong. No major change in policies is expected, but Goh will try gradually to move to a more consultative style of government.

Many of the basic needs of nation-building that inspired the PAP three decades ago have been met, and now, as in the other NIEs, broadening prosperity and education have raised issues of government accountability and greater tolerance of opposing views. However, in contrast particularly to South Korea and Taiwan, the paternalistic Singaporean government has become increasingly heavy-handed. Over the past two years, vindictive attacks have been made on opposition MPs and a former president of Singapore, alleged neo-Marxist conspirators have been detained without trial, the foreign press has been restricted, Malay–Chinese communal relations have been sensitized by ministerial statements about loyalty, and the electoral system has been reorganized in such a way as to weaken opposition parties.[22] As a result, despite the PAP's record of socio-economic achievement, and despite the levers of influence available to it, the level of popular support for the party has been declining – for the first time in the 1984 election and, more recently, in that of 1988.

This has not, of course, shaken Lee's faith in himself. He remains convinced of the vulnerability of Singapore and sceptical about the next generation's ability to protect the values and attitudes that inspired his very real achievements. He sees inner divisions even within the Chinese community, let alone intercommunally. Moreover, although his economic policies and foreign policy preferences place him within the pro-West group, he has recently begun to question the nature of the 'westernization' of Singaporean society, and in 1988 even instituted a survey of the 'national ideology' of Singapore.

Chapter 5

Southeast Asia
Unity within diversity

The region known as Southeast Asia holds out great promise as the leader in societal progress and development in the 1990s for the so-called 'developing' countries of the Third World.* Among those who advocate a pan-Pacific regionalism, it has become almost axiomatic that the grouping known as ASEAN (Association of Southeast Asian Nations, comprising Brunei, Indonesia, Malaysia, the Philippines, Singapore and Thailand) will provide the dynamic for any such movement.[1] The specific dynamism of ASEAN, as an identifiable phenomenon within the wider context of Pacific Asian dynamism, became apparent only in the second half of the 1970s and the early 1980s.

Southeast Asia has not always been viewed in such a positive light. Indeed, in a study published in the late 1970s, the Southeast Asian states were identified as being 'likely to have considerable difficulty in handling internal political problems despite their prospects for continued overall growth'.[2] This scenario, however, was not borne out by events. The uncertainties of the post-Vietnam era and US withdrawal from the region did not lead to a situation of falling dominoes, as had been feared. Instead of degenerating into economic and political decay, instability and obscurity, the non-communist states of Southeast Asia, except for Burma, entered a period of dramatic socio-economic transformation and relative peace and stability.

Why, one wonders, did the departure of the United States, and

---

* By 'Southeast Asia', we mean Burma; the three Indochinese states of Vietnam, Laos and Cambodia; and the six ASEAN countries, Brunei, Indonesia, Malaysia, the Philippines, Singapore and Thailand. Papua New Guinea could possibly qualify to be part of the region and already enjoys observer status in the ASEAN grouping.

the uncertainties that this entailed, not have the anticipated effect? The answer, it would seem, is that the foundations of ASEAN's success in the late 1970s and early 1980s were laid *before* 1975, in the era of 'containment', when the United States devoted all its energies to keeping Southeast Asia free from communism. Thus, when the United States finally did withdraw, the impact was far less severe than might have been expected. One might argue further that the cohesion of ASEAN after 1975 owed as much to a combined commitment to face Vietnam, so as to pre-empt a communist irruption into Southeast Asia, as to any desire to fill the vacuum left by the United States.

Although Southeast Asia may no longer belong to an 'American epoch', as some Indonesians believed after the war, the United States still holds a valuable key to the security of the region in military terms, and acts as a counterweight to other powers, external and internal, in the region; its role as 'policeman' should not be discounted. Southeast Asia, in fact, derives its particular character not so much from its openness to change as from its capacity to flourish under external influences for both its security and its development, while at the same time, paradoxically, it tries to avoid external interference and the machinations of the major powers. The key to Southeast Asia's dynamism, indeed, may lie in its relationship with other actors that are both 'predators' and 'protectors'.

THE REGION, PAST AND PRESENT

The challenge for Southeast Asia is as complex now, in the 1990s, under conditions of relative peace and stability, as it ever was. Militant communism (through insurgency and subversion), ethnic polarization, class conflict and religious upheaval are all still present, while the challenges of political legitimacy, social consensus and economic development are even greater. At the level of inter-state relations, the region is still troubled by political division and subtle quests for regional hegemony, by competing territorial claims and long-standing animosities, not to mention the shifting of the balance of power between middle and major powers, both external and internal. At the domestic level, political stability is increasingly subject to demands that are not only the outcome of economic prosperity and social mobilization, but also an indication of politically mature citizenries. Individual states have adopted different forms of government to respond to these challenges, some-times using a mixture of models, ranging from totalitarian to quasi-democratic.

In a region where the primacy of the 'nation-state' is essential to survival, the contradictory truth of today's interdependent world is that this is a notion that now operates only in limited form. In the age of the information revolution, of rapid technological advance, today's inventions rapidly become yesterday's history. National borders no longer mean what they used to mean, now that they can be so easily crossed by such already commonplace devices as facsimile machines.

At least for the non-socialist countries of Southeast Asia, the outstanding challenge is not merely national survival but also the ability to compete in an asymmetrical, predatory and global system of nation-states that are highly competitive; they must attempt to resolve their domestic and external political concerns in an age of nationalism and internationalism, of open information and global interdependence. The challenge is how to be open while looking inward; how to compete yet cooperate; how to be nationalistic and simultaneously international. From the perspective of the viability of ASEAN, and ultimately of a more cohesive Southeast Asia, it is a question of merging national and regional objectives while being global actors as well. ASEAN's success has been its ability to look forward and interface with the world, a far cry from the isolationist approach of the non-ASEAN countries.

On a socio-cultural level, the forces that shaped the post-colonial order in Southeast Asia continue to operate; the tension between traditional and modernist persists. Even in the ASEAN countries, the open and liberal approach to external influences that was initiated by westernized elites in the first phase of independence cannot be guaranteed with complete certainty to continue, despite increased interaction with the international community over the past decade. As for the non-ASEAN states, demands for reversing 'closed' societies are great, but are continually resisted. The power of nationalist symbols in the region should never be under-estimated; there are signs of the re-emergence of traditional elites, who must now pose a challenge to the westernized leaders, whether Marxist or liberal. Yet the clash is essentially one of values – between modern and traditional, between universal and parochial, between secular and religious, between freedom and control.

In politics, Robert Scalapino observes, in comparing the 1950s with the 1980s, 'the broadest developments are clear; the retreat from parliamentarianism and competitive politics has been widespread in the region, and generally accompanied by an increase in power for the military, shared or otherwise.'[3] Whether civilian or military, it is likely that the region will continue to feature strong national authority in societies that are both open and closed, even as these societies become more pluralistic. At the level of elites, the resolution of conflicting values and approaches is likely to have a nation-building, or 'neo-nationalistic', element, with an admixture of both traditional and modern.

On the economic front, new opportunities in business and commerce have created a class of *nouveaux-riches*, thereby increasing the gap between the haves and the have-nots. An expansion of the economic pie has made it possible for the Chinese (who constitute a significant minority of Southeast Asia) to be part and parcel of the process of development in the region; but their role in societies where nationalism is on the increase will be precarious if their assimilation in these societies is not yet complete. The political role of the state in wealth-creation has been an undeniable factor for the region's (basically ASEAN) development; the problem that governments now face is the potential for class conflict arising out of inequalities in the distribution of wealth, as well as the possibility of political in-fighting. It may be, as some have argued, that the emergence of a middle class will go some way towards reconciling such contradictions.[4] Nevertheless, the need for governments to watch for such inequities in their societies will remain as development proceeds and improved communication increases popular awareness of social, economic and political realities.[5]

MODERN SOUTHEAST ASIA

As a region, modern Southeast Asia is young. Given the travails of post-colonialism after the end of World War II, modern Southeast Asia, as a force in international relations, can be said to have come into being only in 1975, after the end of the Vietnam war and what then seemed the imminent complete withdrawal of the United States from the region. In that year, the region entered a state of division that endures to this day and is likely to persist: on the one side, the non-communist grouping known as ASEAN; on the other, a communist Indochina made up of Vietnam, Laos and Cambodia. A third entity, Burma, remains neutral and apart.

Since independence, the influence of the colonial powers has been replaced by that of four major powers, the United States, the Soviet Union, China and Japan, with India acting as a possible middle power. The influence of these external actors has been multifaceted and complex, fusing political, economic and strategic elements. Nevertheless, to quote Sukhumbhand Paribatra, although in the post-1975 period 'external power involvement would remain a fact of life for Southeast Asians, no single extra-regional major actor would be in a position to exert a predominant influence over the region, and the pursuit of the regional states' own interests, demands, and aspirations would have a much more significant impact upon international politics.'[6]

The region's history falls conveniently into four periods. The first two post-war decades, 1945–65, saw the transformation (both peaceful and violent) of colonial entities into independent states and the forging of new national identities in a turbulent setting. In the next decade, inter-state relations were initiated as the new nation-states adjusted to independence and the challenges of political authority and economic development. In the 1970s, one witnesses rapid economic growth in a major portion of the region as one of the most notable of human conflicts in this century – the Vietnam war – came to a close. Finally, in the 1980s, further adjustments have been made to meet the challenges of economic development, political maturity and inter-state relations – and these adjustments will continue into the 1990s, as the region starts to find its proper place in the world community. In such a scenario, the role of ASEAN, as a resilient and adaptable force, will surely be central.

One of the most striking features of the post-1975 era has been the stark contrast between ASEAN and Indochina in economic and political development. The former in the 1970s was not only a crucible of regional cooperative endeavour, albeit largely in the political arena, but also became one of the fastest-growing areas of the world, attaining an average per capita GNP growth rate of between 6 and 12 per cent. Vietnam, by contrast, as representing Indochina, has continued to maintain the world's fifth largest army (and certainly the largest army in Southeast Asia) and is one of the world's twenty poorest nations. The differences in development of the two groupings are reflected in their intense dislike of each other.

As noted in earlier chapters, the 1983–4 world economic

recession seriously affected the ASEAN economies (with the one exception of Thailand, whose resilience seemed to support the claim of some economists that it will soon be ready to join the league of Asia's four NIEs). Even Singapore, which had recorded the highest growth rate of the ASEAN countries during the first half of the decade, recorded negative GNP growth in 1985 – despite what had seemed a successful earlier strategy of diversification into manufacturing. And even oil-rich Brunei found itself forced to realize that its wealth could not last for ever, and accordingly started to look into sources of diversification for its energy-export-dominated economy.

The mid-1980s were therefore a crisis for the economies of ASEAN. The way they rebounded in the late 1980s was a remarkable demonstration of their resilience and dynamism, and the resoluteness of their political wills.

In large part, ASEAN's economic slow-down in the mid-1980s gave proof of its close and interdependent relationship with other economies, especially with those of the United States and the developed countries. Two elements are important in this relationship: trade dependence and the ASEAN economies' reliance on commodity exports. According to the report of the Group of Fourteen, whose establishment itself symbolized the urgent need to bolster intra-ASEAN trade, ASEAN's trade dependence (measured by the ratio of exports and imports to the gross domestic product) stands at 42 per cent for Thailand, 47 per cent for the Philippines, 50 per cent for Indonesia, 79 per cent for Malaysia, 109 per cent for Brunei and a massive 617 per cent for Singapore. As a whole, ASEAN's weighted trade dependence is more than twice the global average.[7] Hence its sensitivity to global ups and downs. At the close of the 1980s, however, the economies of Malaysia and Singapore showed definite signs of recovery, even giving promise of a return to the high growth rates of the 1970s. While, to a considerable extent, this was due to the influx of foreign investment from the developed countries (principally Japan) and from the NIEs, government policies of trimming public expenditures in these two countries also played a role.

The developments of the mid-1980s pose serious questions for the region's survival in a highly competitive world. The non-socialist countries must resolve the conflict between domestic and external concerns if the development process is to continue. The socialist countries, for their part, seem destined to ever greater stagnation if their present regimes continue along the same path, and fail to take into account the tremendous changes that are under way in neighbouring countries and in the Pacific Rim in general – including, even, China and the Soviet Union.

Economic difficulties, in turn, must be related to newly arising political problems. With the possible exception of Singapore and Brunei, all the ASEAN countries have experienced challenges (in some cases severe) to political authority that have affected their stability. Previously, as in Japan, and perhaps also in Korea and Taiwan, a stable political system had gone hand in hand with high growth rates in what may be termed a context of 'semi-competitive' politics: that is, a context in which political partici-pation is allowed, but only to a limited extent and under conditions of *strong government*. Western-style democracy was, so to speak, turned on its head to suit the domestic context. It is possible to take these ideas further and to say that, in the non-socialist coun-tries of Southeast Asia, a system of 'soft authoritarianism' operated alongside 'oriental capitalism': that is, ASEAN's unique blend of a free-market economy with strong governmental direction (result-ing, at an extreme, in the 'crony capitalism' of the Philippines under Marcos).

There are, of course, significant differences among the authority systems in ASEAN. The military, for example, are in power in Indonesia (even if in mufti) and exert a strong influence in Thai-land; but in Malaysia, Brunei and Singapore they are subordinate to civilian authority. Some degree of political participation exists in the grouping's original member-states, but in Brunei, which is a sultanate, under absolute rule, participation is non-existent or heavily circumscribed.

ASEAN's prevailing pattern of governmental authority and intervention in the economy crystallized into a form which, though not perfect, seemed to work so long as the *international* free-market economy was in good health; once this was no longer the case, the imperfections of the model became apparent. Thus the economic recession of the mid-1980s demonstrated just how vulnerable to international market forces the ASEAN economies had become. Not only did growth rates plummet, but political authority was challenged as well.

Although interdependence with the global economy clearly had penalties as well as benefits, not all the ASEAN countries were hit equally hard; nor were their responses all the same. In Thailand, where the recession was not severe, a rebound in the economy led to more 'civilianization', with the possibility that the coup-ridden political process would become one in which the transfer of power among contending political parties would become the norm, beginning with General Chatichai Choonhavan in August 1988. In the Philippines, poor economic performance compounded the problems of the Marcos government and helped to remove President Marcos from power, thereby allowing a return to democratic rule under Mrs Corazon Aquino. In Malaysia, the severe economic recession gave credence to the critics within the ruling UMNO (United Malays National Organization) party, who used it as an argument against Dr Mahathir's government. In the event, the dissent resulted in a split within UMNO and the formation of two factions: one constituting a new UMNO (which remains in authority), and the other, which calls itself *Semangat '46* ('Spirit of '46'), championing the original UMNO and playing the role of political opposition and contender for power. Even in Singapore, as noted in Chapter 4, the ever-powerful People's Action Party (PAP), in power since 1959, has suffered an erosion of popular support.

The increased tempo of change in the domestic politics of ASEAN countries in the 1980s testifies to a fundamental aspect of economic development: that political awakening – even challenges to existing political orders – takes place in the aftermath of growth. It is also clear that the greater the interaction with the global economy, the greater, too, is the likelihood that such polities become exposed to the notion of political accountability – even if somewhat diluted by the conventional wisdom of the countries concerned.

This does not mean that Southeast Asian political orders are about to collapse or to undergo a serious bout of instability. But they are unlikely to continue in their present form; strong doses of government control and curbs on political freedom are already occurring. In the long run, however, legitimacy will derive from economic success, even if development strategy has to be a political decision.

At a collective level, the Southeast Asian countries cannot escape their regional groupings. But a tension between national and regional concerns cannot be avoided. Although the Indonesian thesis of national resilience promoting regional resilience, and vice versa, has validity, there are bound to be differences over regionalism, dictated by national considerations. One such problem area is the question of regional leadership, and the leadership ambitions (even if muted) of ASEAN members; another, even more fundamental, is whether any kind of regional consensus can, in fact, be created as a durable mechanism for decision-making. For the moment, neither issue is a serious problem, but in the coming years both will have to be addressed. Moreover, ASEAN will have to take into account the possibility of Vietnam's regional hegemony – already an inescapable fact in Indochina – eventually extending over mainland Southeast Asia, irrespective of whether and how the Cambodian problem is resolved.

One indication of the fragile nature of ASEAN as a regional grouping took place in late 1988, when Thailand adopted a new tack in handling the Cambodian issue. The Thai government, under Prime Minister Chatichai, announced that it was more interested in turning the 'battlefield of Indochina into a market-place' than in continuing the present policy of isolation, and began to forge closer relations not only with its neighbours Burma, Laos and Vietnam but also with the Heng Samrin–Hun Sen regime in Phnom Penh. These initiatives, which even included a visit to Bangkok by Hun Sen in January 1989, coincided with the view, first expounded by the Thai military, about mainland Southeast Asia – with Bangkok as its centre – being a *suwanaphume* or 'golden peninsula'. The implications for ASEAN's regional unity, however, were less than clear, although Chatichai's government quickly explained that its 'new approach' had been conducted in consultation with its ASEAN partners.

The Thai move ran counter to ASEAN's policy for over a decade of isolating Vietnam, and guaranteeing its pariah status and therefore economic emaciation – a strategy that, in retrospect, was highly successful. It is hard to judge how much damage Thailand's initiative has done to ASEAN as a regional grouping; but, at the same time, it must be remembered that Chatichai's foreign policy cannot be separated from the intricacies of Thai domestic politics, in this case his majority in parliament and the reactions of the military.

'MAINLAND' AND 'ISLAND' SOUTHEAST ASIA

While it is convenient to view Southeast Asia as being composed of two diametrically opposed political blocs, the region can also be divided into 'mainland' and 'island' Southeast Asia. The former would comprise the Buddhist countries of Burma and Thailand, together with the Indochinese states; the latter would consist of the Malay or archipelagic countries of Indonesia, Malaysia, Brunei, Singapore and the Philippines. Singapore might be viewed as a Chinese enclave in a Malay sea, but its geographical and strategic location makes it very much a part of this sub-region. Indeed, it may even be seen as the hub of 'island' Southeast Asia: the epi-centre of a 'growth triangle' consisting of Singapore, Jahore and Batam island – a concept that surfaced in mid-1990.

There are other possible ways in which to view the region's subdivisions and power-centres; it is the very success of ASEAN that has caused one to overlook alternative groupings. Yet this is no reason to suppose that strong national impulses no longer exist within ASEAN. Thailand's readiness to seek an initiative with Hanoi and Rangoon (Yangon) is surprising at first glance, but only indicates an underlying wish to dominate. Some Thai econom-ists in private discussions have espoused the distinct possibility of a new grouping that would link Thailand with the Indochinese countries (Association of Thailand with Indochina, or ATIC), which appears to be another aspect of the 'golden peninsula' con-cept.

Whereas mainland Southeast Asia has roots and traditions that are culturally binding, irrespective of the Marxist-Leninist regimes of Indochina, cultural affinities in 'island' Southeast Asia are less strong and are complicated by the thinking of modern political leaders. Indonesia, as the largest country in the region, is less susceptible to any grand notion of a Malay hegemony of the region or sub-region, even though it may harbour pretensions of being *primus inter pares*. In a different vein, the notion of a Greater Indone-sia, or *Indonesia Raya*, remains in the memory and experience of its neighbours, for the 1963–6 Indonesian–Malaysian 'Confrontation' has left an important legacy in Southeast Asia's international relations.

In 'island' Southeast Asia, Malaysia and Indonesia may well have a notion of a common destiny based on ethnic affinity, but it is also apparent that this has to be one based on relations between equals. The need for political equality may have meant a sacrifice on the part of some for the sake of regional unity and peace, but it is not lost on the small states of Southeast Asia that international politics are conducted on the basis of big fish being able to devour smaller ones. That analogy has often appeared in the rhetoric of Singapore (most recently after the Iraqi invasion of Kuwait), situated as it is between Malaysia and Indonesia, and it explains, in part, the political affinity between it and Brunei (yet another small state that cannot escape from the geographical reality of its two bigger neighbours, Malaysia and Indonesia). It is not lost, either, on some of its neighbours that Singapore, even as it maintains token Malay symbols of statehood, has 'mandarin-ized' itself (the latest example being the permission for a certain number of Hong Kong citizens to immigrate), and has pursued (like the Israelis) a defence policy of being armed to the teeth, presumably to deter its Malay neighbours.

The tenuousness of the concept of 'island' Southeast Asia is further illustrated by the apparent impossibility of reconciliation between Malaysia and the Philippines with regard to the latter's claim to the Malaysian province of Sabah, or North Borneo. Related to this is the issue of their poorly defined sea-borders in the area of the Sulu archipelago, and the influence of religious differences. Finally, if additional proof is needed, the competing claims over the Spratly islands between 'island' and 'mainland' states show how unrealistic it is to attempt any such differentiation of the region. Perhaps the most one can say is that the forces at work in the region we call 'Southeast Asia' are both centrifugal and centripetal.

EXTERNAL ACTORS

The Southeast Asian countries will also have to face problems in the international arena, which is becoming – if possible – even more complex. Not only will the external actors and forces impact in a great variety of ways on the developmental process of the Pacific Asian countries, but their interactions among themselves will have far-reaching effects. The Southeast Asian countries can only look on in this context; but they cannot escape the aftermath of such interactions, especially of any macroeconomic imbalance on a global scale. Of particular importance is how the United States/Japan economic relationship develops, if indeed cooperation is still possible.[8] The outcome of this particular entanglement will, in turn, affect the Sino-Soviet and Soviet–American relationships.

A potentially very positive influence could be that of Japan. If Japan can find for itself an international role that is supportive of the interests and future of the Southeast Asian countries, especially those of the ASEAN grouping, and if they, for their part, can overcome their fear of a repeat of Japan's militaristic past, then a very fruitful Japan/ASEAN partnership could be forged. On this basis, the role of Japan in the coming years could well be that of a 'facilitator' of progress in the region. The future is uncertain, but it is clear that patterns of relationship have changed, and the *Pax Americana*, which for so long provided a general situation of peace in Pacific-Asia (and the climate for ASEAN advancement), is no longer the force that it was. The question here is how a continuing US presence can be sustained once the Americans have withdrawn, as now seems likely, from their base facilities at Subic and Clark in the Philippines. It may well be that Takashi Inoguchi's scenario of '*Pax Americana*, Phase II' will be the political and security architecture of the 1990s.[9]

The Southeast Asian countries have, of course, attempted their own security arrangements for the region. One of the most notable was ASEAN's proposal for a Zone of Peace, Freedom and Neutrality (ZOPFAN). First expounded in 1971, this concept was supplemented in the mid-1980s by the related notion of a Nuclear-Weapons-Free Zone (NWFZ), put forward largely at the initiative of Malaysia and Indonesia. Similarly, it can be noted that while ASEAN has been advocating ZOPFAN, this has not prevented its member-states, Malaysia and Singapore, from utilizing the Five-Power Defence Arrangement (FPDA), which groups them with Britain, Australia and New Zealand, as a subtle insurance policy against external aggression.[10] Thus, in general, the ASEAN countries have adopted a pragmatic approach in their security relations with major powers.

ASEAN COOPERATION

ASEAN's strength rests more on the commitment of its individual member-states to further their own interests than on any altruistic sense of regionalism. Its 'success story', indeed, may be the achievement of unilateralism within a multilateral framework.[11] In the 1990s, as a former Malaysian Minister of Foreign Affairs noted, it will face a new challenge, as it moves 'from adolescence into adulthood'.[12] As an association of equals whose decision-making is based on consensus and gradualism, there will always be the desire from within to accelerate ASEAN's development, and in the process to overlook the fact that its member-states are relatively young and still pursuing essentially nationalistic goals, especially the daunting task of creating their own versions of the nation-state. There will always be a tension, therefore, between the emphases given to national goals and aspirations and those given to regional ones.

Since its inception in 1967, ASEAN's path as a regional association can be seen in two phases: the first between 1967 and 1975, when it had little to show by way of cooperative achievement; and a second, from 1975 to the end of the 1980s, when it enjoyed a quickened pace of activity, especially in the political arena. Some critics observe that ASEAN is a 'one-issue' organization, its solidarity deriving from its political opposition to the Vietnamese invasion of Cambodia in 1978 and the Heng Samrin–Hun Sen regime in Phnom Penh. In the 1990s, a new phase may be in the making, with a Cambodian solution in sight, the withdrawal of Vietnamese occupation forces from Cambodia, and the beckoning initiatives of a larger-than-ASEAN regional economic association, in the shape of Asia-Pacific Economic Cooperation (APEC). New policy tacks by ASEAN's partners, such as the United States (especially Secretary of State James Baker's July 1990 initiative to withhold recognition of the Khmer Rouge in the Coalition Government of Democratic Kampuchea [CGDK], which ASEAN supports), merely serve to complicate the internal challenges to its unity and cohesion.

If ASEAN presents the key to the promise of Southeast Asia, what then can be assumed of its continued vitality in the face of these challenges of maturity? Furthermore, can its survival be assured as the web of its economic interdependence with the rest of the world continues to widen? Can it compete against protectionist trade barriers? How will it be affected by the remaking of Europe and the decline in East–West tensions? Will it still be able to pursue its quest for a regional order in the rapidly changing strategic, political and economic landscape of the 1990s?

Addressing this last question, Donald Weatherbee suggests rather persuasively that the changing strategic landscape, at both the international and the regional level, puts the cohesion of ASEAN at risk and enhances the prospect of intra-ASEAN conflict:

While we could certainly rule out the notion of 'total conflict' in the ASEAN setting, the basic idea of intra-ASEAN conflict and competition replacing consultation and consensus as new elites seek a narrower vision of national self-interest must be consciously addressed if ASEAN is to survive. ASEAN's best security policy in that event will be the recruitment of a leadership as wise and farsighted as their predecessors.[13]

Inasmuch as ASEAN's primary and explicit goals are economic in nature, it seems certain that more attention will have to be focused on national development in order to cope with the challenges of industrial trade competitiveness. If the past is any guide, ASEAN's survival cannot be premised on economic autarky. ASEAN needs to develop a niche in international trade and competition, but it still needs to rely on foreign investment and aid, while at the same time taking care not to become dependent on external sources.

On the other hand, it seems unlikely that the ASEAN countries can become a free-trading bloc, even though this issue was put at the top of the agenda at the December 1987 summit. ASEAN has made a number of moves in this direction, with such regional cooperative endeavours as the ASEAN Industrial Projects (AIPs), the ASEAN Industrial Joint Ventures (AIJVs) and the Preferential Trading Arrangements (PTAs); but these initiatives have met with little success, despite official pronouncements on their urgency. It is clear that the political will for ASEAN economic cooperation has simply not been forthcoming, and this situation is unlikely to change.[14] Nevertheless, ASEAN has managed to speak forcibly, with one voice, in its dealings on trade and commercial issues with its developed, or third-country, dialogue partners* and with international organizations such as the EC and United Nations Development Programme (UNDP). It seems likely, then, that its future economic dynamism will still rely heavily on its *external* economic relations, especially with the developed countries and increasingly as well with NIEs, such as South Korea (which is now a 'sectoral' dialogue partner).

However, these external economic relationships will come adrift if protectionist barriers, or such trading blocs as the European single market, create difficulties for the penetration of ASEAN

* ASEAN has five formal 'dialogue partners' – the United States, Canada, Japan, Australia and New Zealand – whose foreign ministers attend all the meetings of the ASEAN foreign ministers. It has further 'sectoral' dialogue partners for specific sectors.

goods and services. An ASEAN round-table discussion in early 1989 listed the following global economic developments as presenting both opportunities and dangers for ASEAN's future:

(a) a rapidly changing international geopolitical and economic environment;
(b) the increasing importance of economic over military factors in domestic and international security maintenance and enhancement;
(c) the volatility of the global economic environment;
(d) Pacific growth dynamism;
(e) the emergence of trading blocs (e.g. the European single market and the US–Canada Free Trade Agreement);
(f) the globalization of industrial production and the internationalization of national economics; and
(g) the march of technology (e.g. in micro-electronics, biotechnology and industrial materials).[15]

A similar round table in 1990 highlighted the same issues, but added some further points: the need for a continuing US military presence in the region, the will to forge new relationships (as in APEC), continued political resolve, the need to achieve economic deregulation, joint action on trade issues, a strengthening of institutional networks and a more 'ASEAN-minded' approach.[16]

A proposal has been made to establish an ASEAN–US trade regime,[17] but, again, this relates not so much to general economic issues, as to the ability to act together on any particular issue. However, at the end of 1989 there were renewed calls for a more cohesive Pacific area economic grouping to meet the double challenge of Europe's single market and the North American trading bloc: this resulted in ASEAN's agreement to explore ways of enhancing cooperation with the developed Pacific Asian states through the new network of APEC. That APEC essentially groups ASEAN with its dialogue partners may be an auspicious start, but it also seems clear that, for the time being, APEC will be primarily a consultative process and that the considerations of ASEAN will remain paramount pending further institutionalization.[18]

If ASEAN could achieve so much by way of regional cohesion, why have similar arrangements been less successful? The three Indochinese states, despite their *de facto* federation under Vietnamese hegemony, have had little to show in terms of economic development. But even if not replicable, it is useful to reflect on ASEAN's success, and to observe the workings of an association that has allowed unilateralism to flourish within a multilateral framework, and national decisions to coexist with regional aspirations.

Indeed, the paradox of ASEAN has been that it *does* work: in spite of the fact that it has been unable to achieve sufficient economic cooperation to transcend national trade barriers, in spite of its members being competitors in the economic market-place, an ASEAN spirit of working together pervades decision-making so that, at important moments, it has allowed trade protection for individual member-states (such as the export of Thai tapioca to the EC, tropical-oil lobbying in the United States, and Singaporean air-landing rights in Australia and New Zealand). In all this, it has been assisted by its lack of institutional constraints, by the absence of an overarching secretariat that would have bureaucratized decision-making beyond the primacy of national interests and the spirit of consensus that now rule. It is this looseness of structure that has enabled ASEAN to speak as one voice on issues affecting the stability, politics and economics of Southeast Asia.

Yet another vital key to an understanding of ASEAN has been its ability to adhere to 'codes of conduct' that provide the legal (and perhaps extra-legal as well) bases of its existence as a regional organization. These are essentially its charter, the Bangkok Declaration of 1967, the Bali Concord (signed in 1976) and the Treaty of Amity and Cooperation (1976). It is these codes of conduct which have enabled the ASEAN spirit of working together – a 'state of mind', as a former Malaysian foreign minister, Tan Sri Ghazali Shafie, put it – to prevail and which have provided the cultural underpinnings of ASEAN.[19] In this respect, ASEAN's success is a reflection more of a cultural ethos, or world-view, than a structural format (the latter probably being more important in a 'European' context). Personalities have a role in such a context, but it is precisely for this reason that the continuity of an ASEAN 'value-system' seems an important element for the grouping's continued viability.

ASEAN/INDOCHINA RELATIONS?

In the light of a near-resolution of the Cambodian problem, and Vietnam's withdrawal of troops, the path may be assumed to have been paved for a more constructive regional order in Southeast Asia, especially in terms of ASEAN/Indochina relations. There seemed, at last, to be some prospect of breaking the two-bloc grid that had been the basis of the region's political condition since 1975. With the objective of a more peaceful and constructive Southeast Asia, ideas have been mooted for the expansion of ASEAN to include the Indochinese countries, or, at least, for the formation of an ASEAN/Indochina forum that could link these two sub-regional entities in the political and economic spheres, prior to integration in a more formal institutional framework.

Such proposals, however, call for a genuine meeting of minds, not just a reconciliation of political differences, or even an adjustment of economic strategies. It would certainly be in the best interests of ASEAN to encourage peace and prosperity in Vietnam so that both ASEAN and Indochina could achieve growth on a mutual basis. This is very much like saying that the West should assist President Gorbachev in his *perestroika* efforts so that more stable and concrete East–West relations may emerge.

As discussed in more detail in Chapter 6, the present state of economic stagnation in Vietnam may well require both Western and ASEAN assistance in opening up the economy, as was the case in post-1978 China. In the face of reduced Soviet and Soviet-bloc aid, this is a matter of some urgency, if a complete collapse of the economy is to be avoided. For the moment, however, it should be recognized that Hanoi's economy *is* in a shambles, except perhaps in Ho Chi Minh City and former South Vietnam, where there are signs of vibrancy and economic resuscitation.

But those who argue that Vietnam deserves any help it can get are conveniently decoupling the economic from the political and strategic. In a centralized economy such as Vietnam's, any economic decision is a political decision, and herein lies the most outstanding obstacle to any form of economic recovery. As in other Marxist-Leninist regimes, the existence of a fossilized leadership and stultifying party bureaucracy pose huge obstacles that only a complete dismantling of the regime would finally remove.

Politically, there appears to be no doubt that Vietnam wishes to remain ascendent in Indochina. This means that it will use Cambodia as a safety-belt for its security. That is why, in spite of the troop withdrawals, it has continued to be involved in Phnom Penh's military operations against the CGDK resistance. In other words, caution is needed in dealing with Vietnam, until and unless the regime itself is dismantled. The readiness of some within ASEAN circles to accept Vietnam's moves to resolve the Cambodian issue and generally to seek ways of overcoming its international isolation is probably premature. Efforts have also been made to expand trade and investment links, perhaps in an attempt to ensure that not only Thailand will benefit from the policy of 'turning Vietnam from a battlefield into a market-place'.

Anyone visiting Hanoi will quickly appreciate that abundant business opportunities exist, despite depressing first impressions and decades of neglect. In former South Vietnam, the picture is more tantalizing and hopeful, but, as a whole, the Vietnamese authorities are careful that their relaxation of controls shall not lead to a non-socialist situation. The Vietnamese may appear eager for an opening-up, but, ironically, they know that what really counts will be recognition by the United States, the very country they defeated in war. Small amounts of aid are coming from countries like Australia and France, but until the US 'relents', few international funding agencies will be forthcoming with assistance.

It is startling to note that Vietnam continues to be on a war footing, with troop strengths estimated at between one and one and a half million. It is even more startling to observe, according to information received by the Economic and Social Council for Asia and the Pacific, that the Vietnamese find it 'more economical' to have such a large army than to reduce it. In short, Vietnam faces a real dilemma as it begins to seek a new role for itself in Southeast Asia and the region as a whole. But until it can achieve a certain amount of political liberalization, in order to pursue economic modernization, its accession to ASEAN will be difficult.

* * *

The idea of a unified Southeast Asia linking ASEAN with Indochina and Burma, a collectivity that would transcend whatever political and economic differences had existed in the past, looks like remaining no more than a tantalizing prospect. It neglects *realpolitik*, and above all the obdurate leadership underpinnings of non-ASEAN Southeast Asia. Trapped by their peculiar brands of self-deceiving national independence and vehement resistance to the pace of international change, the future looks dim for these countries if their regimes continue basically unaltered.

As to ASEAN itself, it will have to pay increased attention to outside players – the United States, Japan, the Soviet Union and, to a lesser extent, China. These countries will loom even larger in the political and economic spheres than before, even as ASEAN attempts to forge its own regional cohesion beyond its apparent political unity. Indeed, it could well be that the Cambodian issue will have become less critical, irrespective of whether Vietnam's hegemony prevails. Internally, the ASEAN member-states will have to come to terms with the greater impact of international developments on their domestic policies. The possibility of social and political unrest, as well as questions of leadership, will have to be faced. As each country inevitably becomes increasingly pre-occupied with its own problems, and assumes what Weatherbee calls 'a narrower vision of national self-interest', ASEAN's new, second-generation elites will need constantly to remind themselves to take the long-term view.

Chapter 6

China and the socialist states

The massacre in central Beijing on the night of 3–4 June 1989 had implications whose full scope it is still not possible to assess. China's modernization programme was dealt a blow from which it will find it hard to recover, and its international image was seriously damaged. Despite repeated assertions that its open-door economic policy would remain unchanged, it was clear to the outside world that the Chinese leadership had relapsed into a sterile ideological debate that would inevitably work against the country's economic growth. The scenes of brutal repression that were televised around the world provoked unanimous moral indignation against China's leaders, who were depicted as a group of old doctrinaires ruthlessly protecting their outdated and largely irrelevant power and privilege. Western governments showed little restraint in their condemnation, partly because the China card, once a powerful instrument in global politics, had lost potency in the post-cold-war world.

But it is an oversimplification to see the tragedy purely in terms of the perverse folly of old men. The fact remains that if the leadership had not resorted, at that particular juncture, to a decisive, if deplorable, action against an increasingly unruly mob of demonstrators, the country might have disintegrated into complete chaos and confusion, with untold consequences for the region and the world. Justified as the criticism of China's octogenarian leaders may be, for the means by which they chose to quell the pro-democracy uprising, it is likely that they were as much the victims of an unexpected turn of events as the demonstrators themselves, and that they therefore turned automatically to the course they knew best – repression by force. It is likely, too, that they were well aware that such action would go flatly against the modernization road which they had pursued carefully, and by and large success-fully, over the past decade, and that it would strike a serious blow at the legitimacy of the party and of the government, inside as well as outside the country.

China's clampdown in mid-1989 posed awkward problems of adjustment for the other socialist countries in the region, especially North Korea and Vietnam. Living under the dominant influence of the Soviet Union and China, these two countries have long had to walk a tightrope in order to adjust to the vagaries of the two communist giants. China's sudden shift to modernization in 1978 was highly unsettling for them because it implied that China was calling into question the validity of traditional Marxist-Leninist doctrine, which was, after all, the most important source of power and legitimacy of their regimes. However, the massacre in Beijing's Tiananmen Square, and the restrictions that followed, would hardly have given them any solace either, because it demonstrated the magnitude of the difficulties involved in shifting a centrally planned economy to a market economy, a task that they, too, will have to attempt sooner or later, if they are to avoid becoming totally irrelevant in the years to come – the geese that are left on the ground. This chapter will attempt to analyse the difficulties involved in China's modernization effort, and why the failure to address them could be said to have led to the Tiananmen tragedy, and will briefly consider how the other socialist countries will respond to these changes in the 1990s.

DENG'S MODERNIZATION

The programme of reform launched in 1978 by Deng Xiaoping and the leadership of the Chinese Communist Party (CCP) was, in a sense, a desperate gamble to address the 'equality of poverty' left behind by the Cultural Revolution (living standards were no better than those of a decade earlier), as well as the public's widespread disillusionment with the CCP and its arbitrary and erratic behaviour in the past. The 'class struggle' was implicitly put on a back burner, and was replaced by the goal of economic development as the top priority, in the name of the 'Four Modern-izations'. Agriculture, industry, science and technology, and national defence were to be modernized by the end of the century, with an ambitious target of quadrupling the value of the 1980 gross national output by the year 2000.

In the event, the gamble paid off better than Deng and his planners had expected. Following the introduction of a contract responsibility system into its agricultural sector in 1979, China's economy was consistent in showing robust growth – a demonstration of the outstanding entrepreneurial qualities of the Chinese people. During the period of the Sixth Five-Year Plan (1981–5), grain output increased by 16.6 per cent, resulting in dramatically reduced imports. Cotton production grew by 100 per cent, making China – a long-time major importer – self-sufficient in raw cotton, and enabling the government to lift the rationing of cotton textile.[1] By 1985, China's food imports and exports were roughly equal for the first time since 1949, thus easing the chronic pressure on the country's balance of payments.

With official blessing for farmers to launch a variety of side businesses, there was an explosion of small-scale cottage industries, from handicraft-manufacturing to light industry, from poultry- and fish-farming to meat-processing. The farmers were ingenious enough to raise the investment capital either by borrowing it or by inviting friends and relatives to equity participation. Some obtained trucks and undertook the transportation of the products of the villagers; others acquired tractors and took on, for a fee, work for neighbouring farmers. These activities have created millions of new jobs: 32 million by 1983 and 87 million by 1987, which represented 22.5 per cent of China's 400 million workforce in the agricultural sector.[2]

Industrial and financial reform has been more erratic – and less successful – than rural reform. The intention was to make enterprises more economically responsible through enterprise profit retention, a contract labour system, strengthened managerial (as opposed to CCP cadre) authority and accountability, and, since mid-1987, a contract responsibility system. An enterprise law, which came into force in August 1988, was an attempt to legalize various experiments in managerial responsibility already widely practised in state-run factories.[3] Part of the problem of economic reorganization has been that the state industrial sector still employs more than half of the urban industrial workforce; the government has tried to revitalize the state sector but, consistently since 1980, it has been outperformed, in terms of annual growth of gross output value, by the collective sector.

The successes in the rural economy, particularly, changed China's image greatly. Deng was universally praised as a courageous and far-sighted leader, who had attempted to reform communist doctrine. Perhaps it is not too much to say that China's radical change of direction at that time had the effect of demonstrating serious flaws in communist doctrine and forced the entire communist world to grope for new structures – a process that eventually led to the end of cold-war confrontation.

The impact on the region was equally great. To the other Pacific Asian countries, the economic pragmatism that China suddenly began to embrace appeared to have much in common with their own traditional ethos. Deng's well-known aphorism that the colour of the cat, black or white, does not matter, provided it catches mice, contained a truth that they had long recognized in the name of 'developmentalism'. The sense of optimism that had been building up in the region about China's new commitment to modernization, and its capabilities as a trading partner, was reinforced by the ingenious formulation of the terms that were written into the 1984 agreement with the United Kingdom over the return of Hong Kong. The concept of 'one country, two systems' appeared as the ultimate demonstration of Chinese pragmatism.

HURDLES AND PITFALLS

China's modernization, which began so promisingly, was later to encounter a series of intractable problems and contradictions. The cumulative effect of the leadership's repeated failure to take full account of these, in particular of their political implications, was to culminate, over a decade later, in the tragedy of Tiananmen Square. In retrospect, the success of modernization at its initial stage was received with too much optimism, inside and outside China, largely because of wishful thinking. As a result, the true difficulties involved in grafting an entirely different system onto the inherited economic structure were underestimated. As David Goodman has argued, the Four Modernizations have been neither a blueprint nor a policy for development, but rather an 'aspiration'.[4] The intention was to lift the shackling restraints of the command system and let out economic vitality; difficulties arose because little thought was given to how to control the resulting liberation.

Reform in the agricultural sector was quite simple to set in motion, and thus progressed furthest, since its political repercussions were relatively easy to contain, at least initially. All that the leadership had to do was to replace the traditional system of control over production, by way of such mechanisms as people's communes, with the contract responsibility system, as well as to increase the official purchase price of farm products. In contrast, industrial and financial reform, aiming at making enterprises more responsible through profit retention and strengthened managerial authority, was much more difficult to implement because of its volatile political implications. Moreover, the leadership had neither the experience nor the necessary mechanisms to contain the wild swings of the economy that were to be expected in a market economy, and hence China's economy veered between the enforced retrenchment of 1980–1 and unsustainably high growth, or 'over-heating', as in 1984–5 or again in 1988. Predictably, the reform of the price and wage structure was to become a serious political stumbling-block for the government, as was the question of the privatization of some of the state enterprises.

In fact, these are the kind of problems that all developing economies have to encounter as part of the pain of growth. However, in China, they can easily be blown up, out of all proportion, into the kind of crisis that threatens political stability. This is partly because of the vast size and daunting diversity of the country, which make it quite different from any other country; but, more importantly, it is also because the question of political reform – with which virtually every one of these issues was closely connected – was left largely unaddressed.

THE LEADING ROLE OF THE PARTY

From the very start of the modernization programme, the reformers were struggling to tackle the fundamental question of the dominant, or 'leading', role of the party in the nation's decision-making, and had done their best to separate the party from the state administration. Admittedly, it was a difficult proposition for a regime that was founded upon the sacred premise of the 'democratic dictatorship of the proletariat', and that was able to muster effective violence to stifle any meaningful challenge from the population, to consider the possibility of sharing its power. However, it was becoming increasingly clear that pluralist politics and the sharing of decision-making power with a multiplicity of economic entities, public as well as private, were the essential conditions for the programme of modernization to take root, and for China to recoup at least a portion of its competitiveness *vis-à-vis* the market economies of the region.

Ironically, the problem was aggravated by the very success of modernization. Some of the optimism about China's modernization was based on the assumption that the party machine had been so thoroughly destroyed by the extremes of Mao's Cultural Revolution that bureaucratic resistance to political reform would be minimal, or at least much less than would be expected in the case of other communist countries. Indeed, in the wake of the Cultural Revolution, it appears that virtually all the Chinese people, even seasoned party members, were united in wanting to change the existing system once and for all, and the modernization policy was eagerly welcomed as the only realistic alternative to the ongoing chaos and confusion. Unfortunately, however, the framework of the party's vested interests was revived with lightning speed as soon as national institutions were re-established, even if in rudimentary form, and party members were reinstated in positions that enabled them to take advantage of whatever benefits, economic or political, resulted from the fledgling and yet fast-growing system that was being put together to support the goals of modernization.

As a result, attempts at political reform throughout the 1980s constantly fell short of addressing the fundamental question of the party's role. Raising efficiency, rooting out corruption, overcoming bureaucratic inertia and motivating the masses were all considered admirable objectives of reform, but any suggestion of a reduction in the power of the party aroused the concerted opposition of the rank-and-file party members.

DEMOCRATIZATION AND DEVOLUTION

There is evidence that in the early stages of modernization Deng Xiaoping was aware that China would ultimately need to move towards some kind of participatory government, or 'socialist democracy', and debated with himself on how and when to go about it.[5] It was becoming increasingly clear that one of the fatal flaws in the communist economic system was the lack of freedom in decision-making at each economic unit, from state enterprise down to rural industry. Whereas in the 1950s and 1960s communist countries had been able to record relatively respectable growth, primarily in smoke-stack industries, by the 1970s and 1980s this was no longer possible. A slow-moving and unwieldy central bureaucracy could no longer cope with the sophistication, of production as well as services, of the international economy. Deng himself stated in September 1986 that China's existing political structure did not meet the requirements of economic reform; indeed, 'without reforming the political structure, it will be impossible to safeguard the fruits of the economic reform or to guarantee its continued advance'.[6]

However, although some progress was made in the direction of economic decentralization, political reform did not keep pace, and, for all his insight and political acumen, Deng was never able to take the decisive step that was needed. As a result, he unwittingly promoted the polarization of the Chinese leadership into 'reformers' and 'conservatives'. Although it would be a mistake to think of these as two organized cliques or factions, and although there was no clear policy split between them, but rather a fluid coalescence of opinion which varied according to the issue, there was a constant tug-of-war going on between them. Many of the zigzags in Chinese politics over the past decade can be explained in terms of Deng's manoeuvring from above to maintain a delicate balance – an objective that stemmed, perhaps, from his own, and the party's, deep-rooted fear of losing control.

The fear of decentralization is deeply ingrained in China's traditional political ethos.[7] One of the most important effects of China's open-door economic policy under the reform programme was to give greater say to provincial local authorities and, in particular, to the units of production. But the new pattern of regional economic development also set up new tensions – not just rural versus urban, but between the coastal Special Economic Zones (SEZ) and the inland provinces.[8] One of the major innovations of the Seventh Five-Year Plan (1986–90) was an explicit regional policy which divided China into three main areas: the Eastern Coastal region, the Central region and the Western region. The coastal provinces were to be the focus for export industries and the new knowledge- and technology-intensive industries, the intention being to lure foreign capital and technology to these areas, as well as to sell to foreign markets. In this way, China not only would obtain foreign exchange and technological know-how for free, but would combine a portion of its economy with the burgeoning economies of Pacific Asia. This plan for coastal development caught the attention of the region as being both innovative and economically sound, but it inevitably brought tension with the inland provinces, which feared being left further behind in the race for modernization. As the difficulties resulting from changes in the economic structure multiplied, it became even harder to attempt any thoroughly political reform.

THE CULT OF PERSONALITY

Another – and ever-present – obstacle to political reform has been the in-built penchant of the Chinese people for one-man rule or a personality cult. According to Lucian Pye, 'the Chinese conviction that the power should reside in the central authority – a fact that is acknowledged by the entire population – has been one of the most powerful factors in shaping Chinese history'.[9] Apparently not even the sufferings to which Mao Zedong subjected a generation of Chinese by his reckless launching of the Cultural Revolution were enough to undermine this conviction.

Having seen, and himself suffered from, the madness of Mao's personality cult, Deng was aware of the seriousness of the problem, and tried to prevent it from reappearing, this time around himself, by taking the precaution of not accepting any official position such as party secretary or prime minister, satisfying himself instead with the post of Chairman of the Military Affairs Commission. Nevertheless, as soon as he returned from political exile and helped initiate modernization in 1978, it was Deng who quickly became the ultimate point of reference in China. He must have known that China's tendency to create a centralized-cum-personalized power structure, however deeply rooted in its culture, was not compatible with the country's current pressing need to develop itself as a viable economic entity in the world of the 1980s and beyond.

In the event, for whatever reasons, Deng turned out to be rather susceptible to the pressures that party colleagues, young and old, placed upon him. Despite his conscious effort to have the senior leaders retire, many of them remained in the circle of power and contrived to reassert their influence by plugging into Deng's prestige.

One of the challenges for Deng's biographers will always be to try to follow his thought processes in the crucial years of the mid-1980s, when the fate of China's modernization still hung in the balance. Why did he not give unqualified support to such reformers as Hu Yaobang and Zhao Ziyang, whom he himself had picked out and entrusted with the task of modernization, which, by definition, included political reform? When faced with difficult issues, Deng seemed to refer to his peers, or to make decisions unilaterally, which effectively undermined what precious little political base Hu and Zhao had been able to build up. Perhaps he himself was fearful of letting political reform proceed too fast, which, in turn, may be connected with the intrinsic fear that the Chinese are said to have of decentralization.

MOVING TOWARDS A SHOWDOWN

With Hu's dismissal in January 1987 as a watershed, the reform programme began to be put into reverse. By autumn 1988, the debate about the future course of the economy had been decided in favour of those advocating tighter control and austerity, with price reform being put on hold indefinitely by decree of the Thirteenth Central Committee in September 1988. However, the reformers were able to defend from the conservatives' attack some of their most important schemes for modernization, such as Zhao's own proposal to open up the eastern seaboard for a crash programme of development. At the same time, presumably to fend off criticism from the conservatives, Zhao, in his keynote report at the September 1988 party congress, had to pledge continued adherence to the 'four principles' (first enunciated by Deng in 1979) that form the basis of the 'democratic dictatorship of the proletariat' – in other words, he confirmed the supremacy of the party.

After the death in April 1989 of Hu, who was regarded by the students as a leading reformist, events moved quickly. The ensuing demonstration, initially a gesture of sympathy with the general public, was expanded and persisted, involving a growing number of students as well as citizens and workers. However, the final push was provided in May by President Gorbachev's historic visit to Beijing to mark the long-awaited rapprochement between the world's two largest communist countries.

Deng Xiaoping is reported to have looked forward to this occasion as the crowning achievement of his career. It must therefore have been a source of profound humiliation for Chinese leaders when, at the last minute, the carefully planned programme had to be altered because demonstrators were occupying Tiananmen Square. Matters were made worse by Zhao's widely reported statement to Gorbachev that in China all important matters were decided by Deng.[10] This was an astounding admission for a party secretary, quite unthinkable in the normal environment of Chinese politics. It had certainly not been cleared by the circle of leaders before the meeting took place, and is probably a measure of the state of shock and confusion in which Zhao and the leadership in general found themselves at that time. In a sense it was an admission of the most serious problem in China's political system, namely the CCP's curious inability to manage its own power.

From this point on, the leadership was pushed towards a military clampdown. Even the army group responsible for the security of Beijing and its environs (38th Army Group) was no longer considered trustworthy, and there must have seemed no option but a quick, decisive repression. In desperation, the leadership summoned selected army units from all round the country, with the 27th Army Group from north of Beijing as their core, to form a combined force, which was then let loose on the demonstrators.[11]

CHINA WHITHER?

On 30 December 1990, after a six-day party plenum in Beijing involving 584 senior party members, China announced its Five-Year Plan for 1991–5. In the words of mainland economists, it was a muddled compromise between reformists and conservatives and between provincial leaders and the central government.[12] Plans for cutting government subsidies were withdrawn, despite the heavy burden of offering cheaper food and rent for private citizens and financial aid for state enterprises, while reform of the price and wage structure, as well as of the tax system, was not even discussed. The conservatives were reported to have encountered strong resistance to a full-scale economic retrenchment. However, the administration was unable to offer an effective alternative, partly because of mounting economic ills, such as widespread unemployment, growing income disparities and a draining dependence on state subsidies, but more importantly because of the fear of domestic instability – a fear that seems to have obsessed China's leaders ever since the Tiananmen massacre.[13]

Although the massacre was successful in averting the possibility of a total collapse of the country, it presented China's leadership with so many threats and dangers that it has pushed them into the siege mentality which appears still to be dominating the country's political life. The legitimacy of the party, supposedly representing

China's working masses, was effectively shattered by the use of force against its own people. The cleavage in high places between reformers and ideologues was not solved by the massacre, and there is widespread frustration and inertia around the country, which suggests further, and probably more serious, conflict in the future – a state of affairs that forces the party and the government to be rigidly on guard against the slightest signs of dissent.[14]

Worse still, all this coincided with the collapse in Eastern Europe, in autumn 1989, of one communist government after another, culminating in the grisly demise of the Romanian regime in December. Besides robbing China of the psychological satisfaction of being part of a thriving socialist brotherhood, the developments in Eastern Europe, by implying the *de facto* bankruptcy of socialism itself, imposed a direct threat to the core values of China's communist nationhood. However, there was little that China could do other than brace itself and adhere doggedly to the traditional socialist way. At a party conference in April 1990, General Secretary Jiang Zemin introduced an important 'personal message' from Deng Xiaoping, to the effect that 'no matter how socialism might change its shape in Eastern Europe, as long as China remained committed to socialist ideals, and demonstrated the efficacy of socialism by solving its own domestic problems, there was still hope for it'. Presumably as part of the efficient 'solving of domestic problems', Jiang added that Deng had stressed stability as China's primary long-term political need.[15]

The depth of shock and fear that China felt about events in Eastern Europe was demonstrated in its vehement criticism of Gorbachev, who was painted as a traitor to the basic tenets of Marxist-Leninist philosophy, and as such responsible for the wholesale crumbling of East European socialism.[16] However, in contrast with past times, when China was free to accuse the Soviet Union openly and viciously, it was now obliged to confine these criticisms to the inner circle of its leadership, and had to maintain, at least on the surface, a cordial and business-as-usual relationship, as shown in Premier Li Peng's visit to Moscow in April 1990. The growing difficulties that seem to be pushing Gorbachev to the wall should give some solace to the Chinese as evidence of the fallacy of his new thinking, and as proof of the righteousness of their own attitude. However, this will in no way help them to solve their mounting problems, which stem from the same source, namely 'the irreconcilable desire to have their communist cake but eat a capitalist one'.[17]

It has been relatively easy for China to maintain a friendly façade in its relations with the Soviet Union, because it does not depend heavily on the Soviets in economic terms. In contrast, relations with Western countries are far more complex and difficult because, during the past decade of the modernization programme, economic interaction with the West has become considerable – greater, indeed, than China's conservatives might care to admit. External markets are now vital not supplementary. Exports in 1989 accounted for 22 per cent of GNP, compared with only 6 per cent in 1980. This has, ironically, made the Chinese government more dependent on external factors – factors often beyond its control – than at any other time since the 1950s.

Therefore, although China cited 'interference in internal affairs' in retorting to a barrage of harsh criticism from various Western countries, it was obliged to keep insisting that it would maintain its open-door policy. Moreover, in the hope of inducing a more favourable Western attitude, it has made a series of compromises, ranging from lifting martial law in Beijing and Lhasa (January 1990) and Tibet (May 1990), to the successive release of detainees suspected of leading roles in the Tiananmen demonstrations, to permission for leading dissident Fang Lizhi and his wife to leave the country. Currently it is busily wooing the Bush administration with a view to getting it to contrive, despite stiff opposition from Congress, another renewal of its most-favoured-nation trade status when this comes up for review in summer 1991. However, the leadership has to be very careful not to give the impression of kowtowing to the West, for fear of antagonizing the conservatives in the country. In this connection, China's largely supportive stance towards the United States and its allies in the Gulf war has had the effect of retrieving some of the goodwill lost by the massacre.

In other relations, China was able to bring about the long-awaited 'normalization' of relations with Indonesia and Singapore, while Japan was able to reopen its official aid programme after obtaining tacit approval at the Houston economic summit. Japan's much-publicized $6 billion loan for infrastructure building was finally activated, at least in part, after the January 1991 visit to Beijing of the Japanese finance minister, the first high-level exchange since the Tiananmen incident. Zhao's eastern seaboard programme still seems to attract the keen interest of South Korea, and even Taiwan, while there is talk of major investment to make Shanghai and its vicinity the hub of the entire programme.

It is certainly possible that China can get by, and continue with some growth, for the coming years. However, there is little likelihood of its leadership shedding its current siege mentality and coming up with any imaginative or decisive policy initiative, at least for the present. The leadership will continue to be saddled with a range of contradictions which are bound to make its policy *ad hoc* and reactive. The return of Hong Kong in 1997 is likely to force China to assert its initiative, particularly in terms of economic management, although the scope and extent of such change are difficult to foresee. Needless to say, the most decisive impetus for change will be the demise of Deng Xiaoping himself. However, the effects of the departure of a person with ultimate power on a society like China's are not clear. It is reasonable to expect a great, and perhaps prolonged, confusion, because an orderly succession of power is extremely unlikely in view of the lack of any candidate around whom another personality cult could be formed. And if such a person were to emerge, again it is difficult to foresee whether or not this would be beneficial for China's development, or in what way.

It is, however, unwise to underestimate China. For all its failures and disasters, communist China can boast a record of extremely bold and innovative policies, external as well as internal. One recalls that China was the only country in post-war years that was able to maintain independence from, and was never intimidated by, either the United States or the Soviet Union. Doubtless, its sheer size and potential influence in the Third World was a help. However, it is also true that China was quite ingenious in hedging its seemingly belligerent attitude with a series of innovative diplomatic initiatives. When its vital interests are at stake, it has shown itself able to cast aside past precedents and bureaucratic indecision and pursue geopolitical logic quite ruthlessly, as in its 1971 rapprochement with the United States. Similarly, it has demonstrated in its policies, time and again, its courage in breaking out of the past and experimenting with the future, the latest examples being the Four Modernizations programme itself and the formula of 'one country, two systems', which still has potent implications for Taiwan as well as Hong Kong.

NORTH KOREA

Of all the socialist states around the world that are currently facing grave challenges as a result of the collapse of communism, North Korea's case seems to be a particularly difficult one. Despite its outward appearance of unity and strength, the monolithic political institution epitomized by the suffocating personality cult that Kim Il-sung has built up around himself could prove to be surprisingly fragile and vulnerable – as has turned out to be the case in Romania, for example. Moreover, the highly unconventional attempt to arrange a dynastic succession for his son, Kim Jong-il, does not seem to be building much international sympathy. Although father-to-son succession can work quite well (witness the Chiang family in Taiwan), provided the son has ability and the public accepts him, the Kims' case still appears to provoke a sense of illegitimacy.[18]

In the area of external relations, too, North Korea is running up against a stone wall. Ever since its creation in 1948, the country's survival has depended critically on its relations with China and the Soviet Union. Although there were times when, emboldened by the Sino-Soviet rift, it tried to play one against the other, it was always careful to avoid jeopardizing the goodwill of either. Lately, however, to its dismay, North Korea has discovered that times have changed, and that it can no longer rely on the ultimate protection and support of its giant communist neighbours. For example, in 1990 it could merely look on helplessly as an unusually rapid process of rapprochement between the Soviet Union and South Korea, its enemy-cum-competitor, reached a climax. Presidents Gorbachev and Roh Tae-woo met each other in San Francisco in June, and then again in Moscow in December following normalization of relations in September. Indeed, the callous way the Soviet Union ignored North Korea's displeasure at these moves may be an indication of a long-standing sense of disillusionment with its former ally and protégé.[19]

Likewise, the North Koreans were quite disturbed earlier in the 1980s by China's sudden and all-out move towards the Four Modernizations and the 'open door', which was tantamount to denying the basic tenets of Kim's own brand of socialism – the *juche* philosophy of self-reliance and the foundation of their nationhood. It was therefore with a sense of relief that they learnt of the events in Tiananmen Square and China's subsequent turning-back to a form of conservatism. Hence Kim Il-sung's visits to China in November 1989 and September 1990, and Jiang Zemin's visit to North Korea in March 1990. However, North Korea had to realize that even a 'new China' could not be wholly trusted, given its continuous pushing for economic relations with South Korea and its obvious determination to keep relations with the Soviet Union cordial, if cool, following the rapprochement in May 1989.

Apart from the general decline of socialism around the world, the obvious reason for North Korea's predicament lay in the simple fact that, in an economic context, South Korea, with its burgeoning economic strength, was a much more attractive and important partner to any country, communist or otherwise. It is understandably painful for the North to realize that it has unequivocally lost economic ground to the South. Despite the destruction and dislocation caused by the Korean war, both sides were able to transform backward and war-torn economies into predominantly industrial ones. But the North's statist mode of development, which played a positive role in the early stage of industrialization (until the early 1970s per capita GNP was probably still higher in the North than in the South), is now acting as a serious brake on growth.

Over the past two decades a considerable number of technical experts, many of whom have had some training experience abroad (principally in the Soviet Union), have been admitted to party and government positions. Their concern about the state of the economy has become apparent even from the limited information available from the North Korean media. The Third Seven-Year Plan, announced in April 1987 after a two-year delay, put particular emphasis on expanding foreign trade, but North Korea remains heavily dependent on China and the Soviet Union as trading partners, and, with Western countries still inhibited by North Korean debts outstanding from the mid-1970s, it is doubtful whether targets can be met. Indeed, in 1989 trade totals actually decreased.[20]

In mid-1990, in a desperate bid to gain economic and political recognition, North Korea ventured into a hasty and make-believe attempt at rapprochement with Japan, by way of a carefully engineered move to win over Kanemaru Shin, a powerful LDP politician, who did indeed promise to try to expedite the process of normalization of relations between the two countries. However, despite Kanemaru's somewhat emotional utterances at the time, it is unlikely that the Japanese government will commit itself, during the formal negotiations due to begin in early 1991, to any arrangement which might displease South Korea or the United States.

One possible scenario for the 1990s which might break the impasse and deliver North Korea from the blind alley in which it is caught would be a real move towards reunification with the South. Because the division of the Korean peninsula was in some ways comparable with that of Germany, one is tempted to speculate in terms of the recent unification of Germany, although the political environment in the two cases is of course different. The fact that reunification might very well spell the end of the Kim regime, as was the case with the Honecker government in East Germany, makes the prospect uncertain. Like the two Germanys, North and South Korea have tried their own dialogue ever since 1971. However, these attempts were sporadic, and often interrupted by obstructionist tactics on the part of the North. With its position steadily deteriorating, North Korea is likely to be more careful now to preserve a route for dialogue with the South.

VIETNAM

In contrast with the two Koreas, Vietnam was able to reunify its divided halves as a result of its victory in the prolonged war with the United States. The former leaders of the North were naive enough to expect that once the war had ended with victory, the nation's economy would automatically recover and bring about prosperity to its people, if only as a reward for the hardships that they had endured for so long.

In the event, not only did reunification do little to solve the country's economic problems, but its history after the 1975 turning-point was one of continuous troubles and disappointments. Besides provoking attack by China, which Vietnam could ill-afford to counter, the invasion of Cambodia turned out to be a prolonged and expensive operation, and extremely damaging to Vietnam's international status. To make matters worse, the hasty attempt to merge the northern and southern economies was not only a failure, but a source of many problems, including the embarrassing and continuous exodus of hundreds and thousands of boat people. Fifteen years after the end of the war, the living standards of the

Vietnamese people showed no improvement over those that prevailed during the war.

In the hope of reviving its economy, the Vietnamese government
has been cautiously experimenting with reform. A liberal foreign-
investment law was enacted in December 1987; then, with advice
from the IMF, a strict monetarist policy was introduced early in
1989, which helped to bring down inflation.[21] Reforms have begun
to spread from industry and agriculture into the banking sector
as well. Agricultural reform has had the most pronounced success;
from being reportedly close to famine in some parts of northern
Vietnam in early 1988, Vietnam actually became the world's third
largest rice exporter in 1989. The industrial picture is more mixed,
as many inefficient state enterprises have been left to flounder
while some priority heavy industries continue to obtain subsidized
funding.

In line with other socialist countries, economic reform brought
about routine ideological opposition inside the party and government. The summer of 1989 saw the beginning of a conservative
backlash, with calls for greater controls on the media and better
party discipline, along with forceful criticisms of 'counter-
revolutionaries' in Eastern Europe and China. In response,
Nguyen Van Linh's September 1989 National Day speech made
it clear that no such democratization of the political system was
envisaged, and this line was maintained in 1990. In March 1990
the leading political reformer in the Politburo was sacked, and
arrests of dissidents have been reported.[22] Opposition to reform
comes not merely from senior party conservatives but also from
lower-level party cadres, reluctant to implement changes that could
cost them their existing privileges.

However, the external environment seems to invite the Vietnamese to graduate from these outdated ideological skirmishes and
to get on with the future. Soviet aid, which has long been a
mainstay of Vietnamese independence, militarily and economically, is likely to dry up soon; on the other hand, the United States
indicated in July 1990 that it was now willing to reconsider, and
improve, its relations with Vietnam. More importantly, perhaps,
its neighbours in Southeast Asia are beginning to explore new
relationships with Vietnam. Thailand is keen to establish a working relationship with all Indochinese countries, partly to expand
the hinterland of its burgeoning economy, and partly to secure a
position for itself in continental Southeast Asia. Indonesia, a long-

time friend, seems eager to facilitate Vietnam's entry into non-socialist Pacific Asia, as shown in President Suharto's comments in Hanoi in late 1990 on prospective Vietnamese membership in ASEAN. All this suggests that, in its relations with the outside world, Vietnam is in a far more favourable position than North Korea.

Arguably, if Vietnam can alter its economic system to the extent of making normal interactions with market economies possible, it may be able to establish a viable working relationship with the non-socialist world without changing its leadership, or altering the basic fabric of its nationhood. If it is courageous enough, and far-sighted enough, to move in this direction, it could give a new hope for socialism to survive, and even prosper in the world of the 1990s and beyond.

Chapter 7

Japan as facilitator

There is little doubt that Japan can and should make a substantial, indeed crucial, contribution to the world of the 1990s. Its burgeoning wealth can play a pivotal role in facilitating the global development process, as well as financing US fiscal deficits. It is likely to emerge as an important market to absorb more goods and services from the developed as well as the developing countries. Its ODA expenditure will increase further, while the transfer of its technology may help contain Third World environmental problems. The question is, will Japan be able to make these contributions within a coherent policy framework, and how successful will it be in coordinating its activities with those of others so as to assure the maximum benefit for all?

Unfortunately, Japan seems to have considerable difficulty in developing a genuine sense of responsibility for the region or the world. In its perception, the world has remained essentially a given, a state of affairs that it has to live with and make the best use of, but not something that it has the capacity, or even the qualifications, to help manage. Moreover, Japan has been singularly blind to, and ignorant of, the impact that its success might have on other countries, friends and foes alike. This tendency dates back to the incredible unawareness of Meiji Japan to the kind of strain that its drive for a 'rich nation, strong army'[1] was imposing on the existing world order and balance of power. A similar insensitivity has been shown in its present-day behaviour in regard to its trading partners, particularly the United States. This chapter considers some of the problems that Japan experiences in its external relations, taking its peculiar insensitivity to the reactions of others as a point of departure; then moves on to examine the country's political system and two-tier economy; and, finally, speculates on Japan's prospective behaviour in the 1990s and beyond.

IGNORANCE AND INSENSITIVITY

Japan's post-war development alternates between decades of great economic growth and decades of adjustment. Each decade of expansion bred discord and friction with the outside world, and had to be addressed by the following decade of adjustment. As Japan's economy grew bigger with each cycle, so did the scale of its conflicts with the outside world. This peculiar process seems to indicate that, while Japan was extremely adept at growth management, it was singularly bad at understanding the implications of its own success.

This was, in some senses, a replay of its pre-war performance. As a very late-comer to the modern world, Meiji Japan had chosen to pursue the objective of achieving a 'rich nation, strong army' with full vigour; otherwise, it would have found it difficult even to maintain independence in the nineteenth-century world of colonialism. However, it appears that it had naively assumed that once the country was modernized (*bunmei-kaika*), it would be accepted as an equal partner by the 'developed' West, and would share power and responsibility throughout the world happily ever after.

In a similar vein, Meiji Japan was quite unaware of the fact that its rapid economic growth would increase its resource vulnerability, and that the country would have to embark on the hazardous road of colonialism. However, once it had reached this point, it saw little reason for a 'developed' Japan to refrain from taking the same path as the Western nations had taken. But by the time that Japan launched its colonial exploitation of the region, starting from the Korean peninsula, such behaviour was no longer acceptable to the world. The general attitude towards the morality of colonialism underwent a great change at the turn of the century, and the spectacle of Japan, an Asian country, dominating and plundering its neighbours had a psychological impact that was qualitatively different from any feelings that earlier Western conduct might have aroused.[2]

There is little doubt that Japan's peculiar blindness, or self-centredness, stems at least in part from its geography and history and that these qualities were enhanced by the 250 years of forced isolation decreed by the Tokugawa government. Even after it opened its gates to the world in 1868, the countries outside its borders were judged largely on the utilitarian ground of whether or not they would advance Japanese aims, with little wish or inclination to relate to them for the sake of any common benefit. An age-old tribal habit of dividing the world between 'us' and 'them' has further prevented the Japanese from appreciating the external consequences of their actions. This self-centred thought-process has persisted, despite the series of difficult problems that the country has had to grapple with, and despite the trauma of defeat and occupation.

If anything, the position in which Japan found itself after the war reinforced its tendency to behave as a loner. Its whole post-war development was conceived within its own borders, without reference to whatever else might have been going on in the region.[3] The model of the 'developmental state' that Japan was instrumental in putting together took little account of the external implications of its future success. Likewise, the decision to adopt a growth strategy based on heavy industry failed to awaken the Japanese to the potential hazards of both a resource crunch and trade conflicts. This is not to say that Japan's growth was realized in a vacuum. The Korean war provided the initial impetus for the expansion of its industry; and it took care from the beginning to develop friendly relations with regional neighbours, in the hope of securing markets as well as resources. However, there was no coordination, let alone integration, of its developmental process with that of the region as a whole.

The same loner mentality was reflected in Japan's handling of the legacy of its past. In this respect, the analogy with West Germany is revealing. Whereas West Germany, led by Chancellor Konrad Adenauer, was deeply conscious of the need for reparation, and indeed made it its policy to make restitution for the past and contribute to the future by cooperating with, and even making sacrifices for, the rebuilding of Europe as well as the world, the Japanese were inclined to believe that their war was at least in part an attempt to redress the ills of a world dominated by the West for some 200–300 years. Admittedly, successive post-war governments were keenly aware of how harshly the world judged Japan's conduct during the war, and particularly the massive suffering to which it subjected the peoples of Pacific–Asia. They entered into a series of war reparation agreements, and issued public apologies for Japan's past on a number of occasions; but these were not backed by any policy framework in which systematic restitution could be made. The absence of such a moral undertone from Japan's post-war policies may, at least in part, have caused the persistent image of Japan being reluctant to support the post-war world system, whether in defence expenditure, trade policy or aid to the Third World. If Japan had been willing to face the cost of its conduct right from the end of the war, its perception of the world and its own role in it might have been very different.

Clearly, the 1960s were a decade of spectacular growth for Japan. However, it paid little attention to such world-shaking events as the Vietnam war, which it regarded as merely a 'fire on the other side of the river'. It had little appreciation of the sociopolitical costs of that war to the United States, and therefore was not able to anticipate or understand the basis of a series of trade conflicts that were to dominate US–Japanese relations in the following decade. Likewise, it was quite oblivious to the political implications of its successful economic penetration into the markets of Southeast Asia. Assuming, quite naively, that although its political interference was unacceptable, largely because of its pre-war record, its economic involvement would be tolerated, even welcomed, Japan invested heavily in resource extraction and market expansion, and unabashedly flooded Southeast Asian countries with a range of consumer goods and electrical gadgets – until the violent eruption of anti-Japanese emotions in 1973–4 took it by surprise and shattered its complacency.

Its confidence in unchecked economic growth was shattered, too, by the 1973 oil embargo by the Arab producers. The government tried every diplomatic means to earn the goodwill of the Arabs, who suddenly seemed to possess the power of life or death over Japan's economy, while at the same time setting in motion an extensive nationwide drive to save energy, and reduce production costs. It was successful in both endeavours. The Arabs soon agreed to resume the normal supply of oil to Japan. Japan's energy consumption began to decline dramatically, while conservation efforts resulted in an engineering revolution at virtually every production site in the country, culminating in Japan gaining runaway industrial competitive advantage.

TRADE DISPUTES

There is little doubt that the so-called 'textile wrangle' of 1969–71 was merely the start of the most intractable problem in Japan's post-war external relations. In a sense, this was part of a broader question of how far could, and should, the world accommodate the dynamic process of change in comparative advantage between the developed and the developing economies. In terms of US–Japan relations, it was a question of how far could, and should, the United States tolerate the expansion of Japan's share in its market. Here again, Japan's peculiar insensitivity to the implications of its own activities made the negotiations more cumbersome and antagonistic than was necessary. Unaware of the price that the US economy was being forced to pay for the prolonged war in Vietnam, Japan held an anachronistic perception of US strength which lingered well into the 1970s and made Japanese reactions to subsequent trade issues unrealistic and often over-defensive.

Having grown wiser from its painful experiences during the textile disputes, Japan chose to agree to various novel formulas of compromise, such as the Trigger Price Mechanism (TPM) and Voluntary Export Restraint (VER), during subsequent disputes over its exports of such items as colour televisions, steel and automobiles, which followed one after another during the 1970s.[4] These issues were somewhat easier to handle, since the Japanese government was able to clinch deals through informal consultations with big business, without having to confront the grass-roots interests of small manufacturers, as had been the case for textiles. Moreover, the results of compromise were not all to Japan's disadvantage: the industries concerned were quick to defend their interests, either by shifting production facilities to the United States or by organizing de facto export cartels assuring hefty profits, which were quickly reinvested to improve competitiveness further.

However, when, in the late 1970s, Japan's restrictions on imports, long symbolized by beef and citrus, were challenged by the United States and other countries, the government's tactic of separating the process of external negotiation from the reaction of domestic vested interests became increasingly difficult to implement. Imports, particularly those of agricultural products, were subject to a range of protective regulations that were jealously guarded by the combined interests of bureaucrats, politicians and farmers. Their hand was strengthened by the feeling predominating among the public that the root of the problem lay in the American industry's own decline, and that Japan was being punished for its excellence and hard work. There were few who questioned whether Japan's own all-out, relentless growth might not have contributed to the difficulties in which the United States found itself, or who tried to search for a pattern of behaviour more likely to promote economic stability.

In the event, the phenomenal growth of Japan's exports in the 1980s, and its ever-increasing trade imbalance with the United States, led the US administration to try not only to reduce trade deficits but also to change some of the basic furniture of Japan's post-war system. Although the administration's primary aim was to defend and promote US economic interests, many of the issues raised in the process were ones attributable to the latest changes in Japan's economic structure and, therefore, should have been addressed by the Japanese themselves without outside pressure. For example, the surge of Japan's high-technology manufacturing since the end of the 1970s, due primarily to its ever-improving engineering prowess, should have indicated to the Japanese that their 'catching-up' period had come to an end, while the pervasive glut of natural resources demonstrated that the country was now liberated from the 'big population, meagre resources' syndrome that had tormented it since the Meiji era. It was obvious that Japan's traditional orientation of exporting more and importing less was quickly becoming not only out of date but counterproductive.

In an effort to overcome the mounting difficulties in Japan's external relations, the Nakasone administration (1982–7) tried to improve the country's image by, on the one hand, redefining its position and role in the world and, on the other, overhauling the post-war political system and restructuring the economy. Unfortunately, all attempts at domestic reform invariably ended up in a tug-of-war between sectoral egoism and national interests.

THE POLITICAL SYSTEM

The merger in 1955 of Japan's conservative political forces, under the banner of the Liberal Democratic Party, had been designed primarily to counteract the campaign that the leftists, led by the Japan Socialist Party, were conducting against the government's conservative, pro-US and free-economy orientation. Although the JSP subsequently proved to be singularly inept at adjusting to the changing needs of Japanese society, the fierce confrontation with the leftists that had taken place in the spring of 1960, which led to the cancellation of a visit by President Eisenhower and the toppling of Prime Minister Kishi Nobusuke, remained fresh in the memory of LDP governments. As a result, a series of administrations maintained a policy of avoiding controversy, ideological or otherwise, by adhering to 'low-posture' politics – a phrase coined by Ikeda Hayato, the prime minister who succeeded Kishi. Although this cautious attitude drew criticism from inside and outside the country, it in fact matched the prevailing mood of the people, who were tired of the sterile disputes of the preceding decade and eager to get on with the practical business of economic recovery.

The LDP's conduct of industrial policy was both effective and astute. Rather than involving itself directly in the details of policy-making, it quietly lent its support to the vigorous programme of measures that the government had set in motion with a view to building up industrial competitiveness. This programme, which resulted in a unique government/industrial sector partnership, was directed, in the main, by the Ministry of International Trade and Industry (MITI). Instead, the LDP, for its part, chose to turn its attention to the 'weaker' sector (such as farmers and retailers), to which it gave pervasive 'care' and 'support' through subsidies, tax concessions and protective legislation against the possible encroachment of big business, domestic or foreign, into its territory. This strategy had the additional advantage of pre-empting the leftists' favourite platform of 'protecting the weak'.

As a result, Japan soon evolved a two-tier economy: the industrial sector, which was open to free, and often fierce, competition inside and outside the country, and a protected sector, which was carefully shielded from competition. In a sense, this was an ingenious formula for enjoying the best of both worlds. On the one hand, it enabled the country to achieve robust industrial growth, which continuously added value to the economy; on the other, it provided the government with a means of ensuring that the fruits of this development reach the 'weaker' sector relatively quickly, and thus of maintaining social stability. Though advantageous up to a point, this arrangement nurtured a potential source of trade conflict, as was shown all too clearly in the comprehensive demands that the United States made upon Japan in the so-called Structural Impediments Initiative (SII) talks in 1989–90.

The issue of market liberalization highlights the curious inability that the LDP has shown to give proper political leadership. This weakness stems in part from the party's factional structure, 'perfected' by Prime Minister Tanaka Kakuei (1972–4). Drawing on his considerable political acumen, as well as financial resources, Tanaka developed an effective formula for extending collective assistance to the Diet members in his faction, meeting their every need, ranging from raising money for campaign finance, to mobilizing connections for personal advantage, to obtaining the government's favour for their constituencies. As a result, the other factions were forced to consolidate their positions, if only to fend off Tanaka's pressure, so relegating the LDP to little more than a collection of different factions, each headed by a prominent politician.[5]

In a sense, this formula was an effective means of maintaining a checks-and-balances system within a party that was perpetually in power, and it compensated for the absence of a credible opposition. But the competition among the factions took a heavy toll in that it immobilized the party's decision-making process. With the real power resting more with the factions than with the party, the official party platform became merely an abstract guideline, leaving the implementation of policy to the mercy of the factional balance of power.[6]

Miki Takeo, Fukuda Takeo and Ohira Masayoshi, successive prime ministers during the 1974–80 period, all did their best to develop comprehensive policy frameworks in order to address the problems of external relations. The so-called 'Fukuda Doctrine', which was made public in Manila in 1977, is still regarded as the guiding principle of Japan's Asia policy, while the comprehensive security concept sponsored by the Ohira administration has remained one of the pillars of Japan's national policy. Ohira's other contribution, a proposal for Pacific Rim economic cooperation has drawn lasting interest from the countries in the region. None of these three men, however, was able to grapple with the basic ills of the nation's political system, because, coming from the lesser factions, their positions depended heavily on the party's factional balance of power.

In 1982, after two years under the somewhat ineffectual administration of a compromise candidate, Suzuki Zenko, the LDP swung to the more vigorous premiership of Nakasone Yasuhiro. Nakasone was fortunate in that, owing to the sudden illness of its leader, the once monolithic Tanaka faction began to lose much of its influence soon after he came to power. With his position thus strengthened, Nakasone was able to embark on an ambitious programme both at home and abroad. His personal rapport with President Reagan, in particular, greatly enhanced Japan's international standing.

In domestic politics, it was clearer than ever that Japan needed to reorganize its entire political system, and that, in order to do so, it needed to have a strong and unified administration, whose commitment was to serve national, rather than sectoral, interests. Throughout Nakasone's five-year term, every effort that he made to mitigate the worsening trade disputes ended up in a battle against the stronghold of vested interests – clear evidence that what had once been the LDP's remarkable efficiency in engineering Japan's economic growth had become a liability where external relations were concerned. Each and every trade liberalization proposal was sabotaged by ministries loath to lose their power and influence. Moreover, there was an unwritten but firm understanding between the ministries involved to respect each other's territory, which effectively left the administration to fight a lonely battle against the combined interests of the LDP, the bureaucracy and the private sector. That was perhaps the logic behind Nakasone's long-term commitment to administrative reform – an area in which he scored his most remarkable successes, such as the privatization of the tobacco monopoly, telecommunications and the railways. Riding in part on these achievements, Nakasone led the LDP to an unprecedented election victory in summer 1986, when it landed over 300 seats in the Lower House.

Unfortunately, soon after, virtually all the leaders of the LDP, including Nakasone himself, were to be caught up in the Recruit scandal, involving privileged share-dealing, which not only put an end to Nakasone's idea of overhauling the post-war system, but undermined his own political base. In fact, the LDP's money politics stems from the extraordinary amount of funds its Diet members need. Even a novice member has to raise at least Y100 million a year in order to run his offices, pay his staff and fraternize with his constituents. Apart from the salary and subsidy for secretarial expenses, which are offered by the government, these needs have to be met by corporate donations, proceeds from the fund-raising parties, and hand-outs from the faction to which the politician belongs. Without doubt, many of them are above board, but some are outright illegal, and many fall in a grey area in between.

In spite of his reputation of being better suited to domestic affairs than to global diplomacy, Takeshita Noboru, who succeeded Nakasone, chose to make the slogan 'a Japan that can contribute to the world' the theme of his administration. He was true to his word. He was able to achieve trade liberalization on many key items, including beef and citrus, which had long been a thorn in the flesh of US–Japanese relations; and he took a number of bold steps in the area of development assistance, pledging substantial increases in Japan's ODA expenditure, promoting the 'Multilateral Aid Initiative' for the Philippines and putting forward a creative programme to recycle Japan's surpluses in order to ease Third World debt. He was helped by his not inconsiderable personal influence, and also by Japan's changing economic environment, which had begun to convince the public that Japan could no longer live by exports alone, and that it needed to survive and prosper in an interdependent global economy.

It was therefore unfortunate that Takeshita's term was cut short – by the Recruit scandal – just when his initiatives were beginning to take root. If Takeshita was brought down by the Recruit scandal, a minor sex scandal caused the downfall of Uno Sosuke; and, in the July 1989 Upper House elections, the LDP lost its overall majority for the first time ever. The party conducted a desperate search for an untainted leader before coming up with Kaifu Toshiki, a relatively young (by LDP standards) politician from one of the smallest factions.

The 1980s ended with three successive years of 5 per cent GNP growth – Japan's best record since the pre-oil-shock years – but the country's confidence in its burgeoning economic power was to be shaken by the steady decline in stock prices since early 1990 which reduced the capitalization of the Tokyo Stock Exchange by a massive Y200 trillion, nearly a half of its value, within a year. Clearly, the extraordinary benefit of the 'three lows' – cheap oil, low interest rates, and a high yen – which had produced the spectacular growth of Japan's current-account surpluses, had come to an end. Although it was never really expected that the abnormally bullish market at the end of 1989 would last very long, it was a sobering experience when the crash became a reality. It deflated some of the self-confidence of the Japanese, whose pride was doubly hurt by seeing that the drastic fall in Tokyo hardly caused a ripple in other markets around the world.[7]

One merit of this downturn was that it put a curb on excessive investment and let some steam out of the economy. More importantly, it was instrumental in changing the outlook of the public, who now realized that the latest market plunge was at least in part a reflection of the political stalemate that had delayed the reform of outdated regulations which effectively insulated Japan's economy from the outside world. Media arguments that the time had come for the country to open its system to more competition and products from outside, if only for the consumer to enjoy living standards that matched the country's wealth, provided the LDP with the support that it needed. It was now able to make last-minute efforts to overcome resistance and push through a solution to the issues blocking the SII trade negotiations with the United States.

Thus, President Bush's invitation to Prime Minister Kaifu to visit Palm Springs, California, for emergency consultations, right after the February 1990 Lower House elections, was timely; and his subsequent move to enlist former Prime Minister Takeshita to back up Kaifu in his struggle to put together an acceptable package back in Tokyo was equally effective in giving new impetus to the government's endeavour. As a result, the US administration decided to drop Japan from the list of unfair traders qualifying for punitive action under the 'Super 301' clause of the 1988 Omnibus Trade Act. Not only was this a great relief to Japan, but it suited the purpose of the Bush administration, which was obviously loath to dwell on the long-standing 'Japan problem' when such pressing matters as Third World debt and the impending Uruguay Round of GATT negotiations, to say nothing of the Middle East crisis, were clamouring for attention. As the US Trade Representative, Carla Hills, put it, the United States preferred cooperation to confrontation in its relations with its trade partners.[8]

AGENDA FOR THE 1990s

It is obvious that the sheer size of Japan's economy has made its inward-looking stance no longer tenable. However, deep down in its heart, Japan is still under the spell of fear and hesitation about exposing itself to the complex world of international politics. In effect, there are a number of factors that would prevent Japan from taking a major political role, either in the region or in the world, even if it wanted to. These can be classified under four main headings.

(1) Lack of leadership qualities

In his article about Japan as an 'underdeveloped international state', Richard Mathews of the *Atlanta Journal* put together the results of in-depth interviews with some 80 Japanese people, each involved in the country's decision-making in some way or other, who had been asked to identify the conditions that would qualify a country for global leadership.[9] The following list emerged:

(a) a large and open market;
(b) substantial natural resources;
(c) nuclear armaments;
(d) a globally acceptable currency;
(e) an international language;
(f) a globally acceptable legal system;
(g) an ideology or well-defined goal;
(h) a group of countries willing and eager to support its initiatives.

Predictably, the United States appears to be amply qualified to be a world leader, while Japan cannot satisfy any of these conditions, with the possible exception of (a) and (d); and it will have to work hard to achieve even these two. To Mathews' dismay, virtually all of his interviewees were of the same opinion, stating that Japan was supremely lacking in the necessary qualifications, and that its people were the least inclined to covet prominence through political leadership.

(2) Japan's unchanged post-war position

Japan's passive attitude can be traced back in part to its anomalous position in the post-war system. Whereas West Germany was given a proper place and role in post-war Europe, no such regional structure developed in Pacific Asia. As a result, Japan's re-entry into the international system was never 'officially' accepted, or legitimized by the nations in the region. Admittedly, many signed the 1951 San Francisco Peace Treaty. However, they did so not

from a genuine wish for Japan's participation, but rather to co
cede to the request of the Americans, on the understanding that
the United States would keep a tight rein on Japan's activities
thereafter. In other words, Japan was readmitted to post-war Asia
on probation, to be sponsored and supervised by the United States.
Unfortunately, this arrangement has reinforced, on the one hand,
the tentativeness of Japan's attitude to the outside world, and, on
the other, its pervasive dependence on the United States.

Surprisingly, the same basic format (which fitted in rather well
with Japan's mood at the time) has remained in place for four
long decades. This was partly because there was no need for a
substantive Japanese involvement in the region's politics while the
United States was a willing and capable guardian of peace and
security. It may also be attributed, however, to the fact that the
nations of the region themselves preferred to maintain this convenient set-up for containing Japan's unpredictable potential. They
have always been careful not to express a genuine appreciation of,
let alone respect for, Japan's subsequent spectacular economic
success, presumably because they might thereby confer a new
legitimacy upon Japan and let it out of the 'cage'. In a similar
vein, the Pacific Asian countries are inclined to underrate the
magnitude of the role that Japan has played in developing the
region's economy, while being quick to point out its shortcomings.
Understandably, this was not conducive to re-establishing Japan's
confidence and legitimacy. However, for its part, post-war Japan
has learnt to live and thrive as a 'second-tier member', which
implied less responsibility but more freedom to pursue its own
objectives. Confidence was recovered with its increasing economic
power, but pride did not seem to bother the country very much.
For example, there was virtually no manifestation of nationalistic
indignation at the time of the anti-Japanese riots in Southeast Asia
in 1973–4, even when the prime minister was mobbed in the streets
of Jakarta.

(3) The Peace Constitution and the US–Japan Security Treaty

Another factor that made Japan's position unique was its security
situation. Japan declared in its post-war constitution (1947), which
was authorized, if not authored, by the US occupation authorities,
that it would never resort to armed struggle to solve problems
in its external relations, and denied itself the right to maintain

military forces. Although the latter clause was reinterpreted later, in part at the request of the United States, in order to allow Japan to build its Self-Defence Forces, a range of stringent restrictions was imposed subsequently by such parliamentary resolutions as the three nuclear principles (not to possess, build or introduce nuclear arms), the ban on weapon exports, the ban on sending armed contingents abroad, and the ceiling on defence expenditure at 1 per cent of GNP.

There is little doubt that the pacifist orientation of Japan helped to allay fears of its remilitarization, and thus contributed to the region's stability. The ban on weapon exports, moreover, precluded Japan from competing in the arms trade and thereby helped to prevent another form of conflict with the United States. On the other hand, these prohibitions put effective constraints on Japan's foreign policy options. For example, its hands were tied by the ban on sending military contingents abroad when it considered how to participate in collective security operations in the Persian Gulf, first in 1987 and then again in 1990. On many items on the international agenda, including the multilateral negotiations on Indochinese problems, Japan has virtually no bargaining power except the offer of economic aid.

More importantly, the no-war constitution, only viable under the US guarantee of Japan's security, resulted in Japan's pervasive dependence on the United States under the terms of the US–Japan Security Treaty (1951), which has become the foundation of the country's subsequent security and prosperity. The Deputy Director-General of the Japanese Defence Agency, Nishihiro Seiki, contends that, besides guaranteeing the physical security of Japan and its environs, the treaty supports the nation's global activities, by way of consolidating its allegiance with the free-world system, and at the same time watches over it so as to prevent it from ill-advised adventurism.[10] Clearly, his first point confirms that Japan's post-war probationary status is still in force, and that its international legitimacy depends critically on its staying under US political influence. His second assertion not only implies that the treaty helps to allay lingering fears in the region about Japan's militarism, but also acknowledges a deep-seated uncertainty on the part of the Japanese about their ability to control their military forces, which goes back to their wartime experience.

In fact, much of Japan's pacifism is attributable to a prevalent doubt, or paranoia, about its own capacity to make the military conform to the nation's political direction – emotions that once again came to the fore as the Japanese government debated the possibility of sending peace-keeping forces to the Middle East in the summer of 1990. Similarly, although public opinion polls show a grudging acceptance of the current level and structure of the Self-Defence Forces, there is strong resistance to any idea of expanding them or using them overseas. As the Middle East crisis has shown, regional clashes are still likely to occur in the post-cold-war world. It is important for Japan to overcome its acute self-doubt about its own military, if it aspires to participate in international politics as a free and independent nation.

(4) The relationship with Asia

Another – more difficult – hurdle is Japan's relationship with Asia. Its callous, selfish and cruel past behaviour towards neighbouring nations still haunts it in its relations with the region. The gross distortion in its attitude towards Asia dates back to the turn of the century. Elated by the victories over China and Russia, Japan began to feel that it had a right, even a responsibility, to exploit the wealth and resources of its neighbours, in order to expand its power further and act as the defender, if not the master, of the region. In a sense, this view was intellectually reinforced by the 'Quit Asia' philosophy propounded by the Meiji scholar Fukuzawa Yukichi, which implied that Japan should apply different standards towards the West and the East, deferring to the former while holding the latter in contempt. As a result, the Japanese developed a completely unfounded sense of superiority towards their Asian brethren, which led later to incredibly mean and cruel behaviour towards people under their power. Apart from the lasting bitterness that this created towards Japan, the Japanese themselves were to experience a moral and psychological trauma arising from their own past.

Popular emotion against Japan still functions as an important determinant in regional relations, in that every hint or insinuation about their past makes the Japanese wince. Whenever difficult issues arise in bilateral relations, be they the trade imbalance, questions of aid or relations with a third country (i.e. Taiwan in China's case), let alone the explosive ones that directly relate to Japan's past, such as the proposed revision of school textbooks or the funeral of Emperor Hirohito, the emotional legacy looms up to strain negotiations.

It is a pity that the uneasy relationship with other Asian countries tends further to complicate the question of Japan's identity as well as its long-standing ambition to play a mediating role between the Eastern and the Western cultures. Being the first non-Western country to succeed in catching up with the West, Japan has long thought that some of its experience might be put to use in smoothing out the encounter between the two. But, before it can do this, it has to clarify its own identity. A top Tokyo business executive is of the opinion that other Western nations are not truly ready to accept Japan as one of the Western leaders, while a former ambassador to the United Nations says that the Asians 'do not really think Japan is part of the East'.[11] This suggests that, instead of mediating, Japan is likely to find itself in the uncomfortable position of being simultaneously rejected by the West and expelled by the East. The only way to get around this difficulty, perhaps, would be for Japan to assume a facilitating, rather than a mediating, role. This would entail extending assistance to both the East and the West, and creating a policy framework for the purpose.

JAPAN AS 'FACILITATOR'

In view of all these constraints, it is not likely that Japan will aspire to an active international role in the early 1990s. Too many problems, many of them the legacy of history, are left unaddressed. There are those who argue that these so-called legacies from the past are no more than excuses for the Japanese to duck their responsibilities. However, Japan cannot commit itself to the future before it clears out the debris of the past. But perhaps the decade of the 1990s will see it graduate, at very least, from its second-tier status, which in a sense it had itself chosen to prolong, and begin to explore different and more positive roles.

The most likely direction for Japan to take is to 'facilitate' the international development process by mobilizing its economic resources, and putting them into action on its own initiative, rather than as a ploy to fend off outside criticism. Japan has long been conditioned to challenge, rather than to facilitate, the existing state of affairs.[12] The first such challenge, made in the Meiji era, was aimed at the virtual domination of the world by the West, and ended in disaster. The second, this time aimed at Western economic supremacy, started up in the 1960s and was successful enough to put an end to such pursuits. Further exercises of 'challenge' will be counterproductive, if not destructive, both for Japan and for the world at large. Clearly, the time has come for Japan to change its orientation and move on to being a 'facilitator' – a role that not only will benefit the world community generally, but will underpin its own prosperity.

In the realm of international politics, Japan will still have to defer to and move alongside the United States, cooperating with, or indeed 'facilitating', American objectives. With the sudden demise of communism, the United States is now the only real superpower, and its policies will have profound implications for the entire world, and particularly for Pacific Asia, where it has acted as a guardian-cum-anchor of stability since the end of the war. While it is too early to speculate on US policy in the post-cold-war world, the United States is not likely to give up its position and withdraw to the Western hemisphere. Pacific Asia's current economic dynamism will remain an important asset to the United States, which is better qualified to benefit from it than any other country outside the region. The region, too, will need the continued presence and involvement of the Americans as it searches for a new political structure in the fast-changing world. Japan can play an important role in encouraging US involvement in the region by building up a viable and equitable framework of burden-sharing. Though still fearful of exposing themselves to the 'real world', the Japanese have little objection to the country playing a facilitator role.

Japan's ODA, which is obviously one of the most important instruments of its facilitator function, has not only been expanded in size, but also been given an increasingly prominent place in Japanese foreign policy. Partly because of the absence of other political means, ODA has been regarded as a major foreign policy instrument ever since the 1970s, when Japan began to use it for a variety of purposes.[13] The large-scale assistance given to Indonesia for the Asahan aluminium and the Arun LNG projects was designed to secure resources, while the aid given to Egypt for the redevelopment of the Suez Canal was a ploy to court favour with the Arab countries, with future oil supplies clearly in mind. The $1 billion package for ASEAN industrial projects in 1977 was conceived in part to mollify Southeast Asia's anti-Japanism. Since the early 1980s, aid for China became an important expression of Japan's support and appreciation of that country's astounding shift towards a market economy. Also at this time, Japan increased its aid to such countries as Pakistan, Egypt and Turkey, primarily to underpin US strategic purposes; and later in the decade it launched a substantial scheme for recycling its trade surplus, in support of US Treasury Secretary Nicholas Brady's ambitious programme to ease Third World debt.

Even under the austerity budgets of the early 1980s, ODA has enjoyed a steady increase, reaching a level of $10 billion in 1990, thus making Japan the biggest aid donor in the world. This is almost the only budget outlay that draws little opposition from the public. On the other hand, Japan has often been criticized for the quality of its ODA, notably as regards the proportion of tied loans to grant elements. While the grant element is indeed being increased significantly, the Japanese tend to believe that a loan is not necessarily less effective than a grant, since it forces a certain discipline on the recipient, which can often be helpful in the developmental process. In the coming years, however, Japan must seriously address its extremely inadequate aid infrastructure in terms of manpower, training, and knowledge of the recipient economies.

Another important facilitating function would be for Japan to expand its market and absorb as many manufactured imports as possible, particularly from developing countries. This has traditionally been considered difficult, given Japan's perpetual need to save foreign exchange in order to pay for the import of natural resources – an argument that has long been used to justify its protectionist leanings. Here again, however, Japan's perceptions are rapidly changing, partly because the latest technological advances have made the country considerably less vulnerable to resource shortages, and partly because the rapid globalization of its economy is making its welfare contingent upon the stability and growth of its trading partners. In fact, Japan's imports have grown so fast in the past few years that its trade surplus in 1989 went down to a mere 1.5 per cent of GNP, a huge drop from 4.5 per cent in 1986.

This leads to the question of Japan's role as a capital supplier. For the past decade, Japan has been financing up to 30 per cent of the US budget deficits, in addition to acquiring a host of other financial and real assets in the United States, Europe and Asia. In fact, it emerged as a major player in the post-war world's third and latest cycle of capital exportation. In the 1950s, it was US capital that financed the reconstruction of the war-torn economies of Europe and Japan. When that flow was stalled by the budgetary and fiscal difficulties that the United States encountered in part as a result of its Vietnam war expenditure, it was replaced by the OPEC oil producers, whose money – recycled primarily through the world's financial institutions – actually aggravated the Third World's debt crisis. When oil prices fell in the 1980s, it was Japan's turn not only to finance the fiscal deficits of various countries but also to build or rebuild productive facilities in the United States, Europe and Asia.[14]

In the end, Japan's ability to facilitate depends on its own economic performance. Barring an unforeseeable catastrophe, its current strength is likely to continue for some time to come. The massive investment being made in technological research and development will probably sustain industrial competitiveness, and hence a reasonable increase in export earnings, for at least the rest of this century. Its energy conservation and diversification programmes have enabled it to be more relaxed about the 1990 oil price rises than was possible for those of the 1970s. The challenge of the fast-growing Pacific economy, with its dynamic and continuous shifts in comparative advantage, will be of help – by way of keeping Japan constantly on its toes. With its current-account surplus in sharp decline, its capital surplus may not last for long. Instead, Japan may soon emerge as a major world importer. The vigorous outsourcing strategy that its industry has been carrying out will serve to reinforce this trend. The capital surplus will be further absorbed by increased spending on the country's infrastructure, partly to meet the demands of the United States under the SII, as well as by the expanding needs of an ageing population.

It will take, therefore, clearly defined policy priorities as well as political will for Japan to consider playing an effective facilitator role. If it can summon the energies to do so, a range of benefits will fall to it – without provoking either external envy or internal resistance. Above all, the role of facilitator would answer the perennial criticism of Japan the free-rider. The frequent complaint that Japan is constantly drawing benefits from the world economic regime while contributing little to its maintenance has been a difficult one to counter. By expanding its role as facilitator, Japan can meet many of these criticisms, and at the same time may even be able to find a legitimate position for itself in the world order, thus filling a singular void in its post-war life, namely the lack of any clear goal or purpose as a nation. The pre-war objective of 'rich nation, strong army' was prompted by the ambition to join the ranks of the leading nations of the world. By contrast, the post-war endeavour for economic development lacked any aim beyond that of improving the nation's own living standards.

In a similar vein, Japan appears to have utterly no idea how it should use its military capability, even though it is endowed with an ever-increasing budget appropriation, designed in part to placate the United States. The internal debate about revising the constitution, generated by Western requests for active Japanese participation in international action against Iraqi aggression in mid-1990, exposed not only the sensitivities of the Japanese, but the immaturity of their thinking as regards Japan's security role. Former US Secretary of State Henry Kissinger has contended that Japan must sooner or later come round to building a military capability commensurate with its economic power, because history tells us that no nation is able to remain an economic power for long without becoming a military power as well. For the present, however, Japan seems to be out to defy the rules of history by being unable to become a military power despite having the necessary capability.

Few nations have ever taken the job of facilitating others as their primary role, even if the outcome may eventually serve the facilitator's own interests. Perhaps the 1990s will turn out to be the decade when Japan learns how to perform this function both gracefully and effectively, and in the process will find the means of achieving moral and emotional reconciliation with its past. Only in this way will it ever find its rightful place in the world. In all likelihood, however, Japan's future activities will be low-key, economy-oriented and essentially a gradual extension of its current facilitating activities. Although this may not satisfy Japan's chauvinists on the right or its pacifists on the left, one hopes that such a course will mark the beginning of a new Japan which, in its own fashion, will contribute to a stable international environment.

Chapter 8

Pacific Asia in the 1990s

As Pacific Asia enters the 1990s, economic development proceeds at such a pace that the countries of the region experience both the pleasures and the pain of industrialization, democratization and, to a superficial degree, westernization. At the same time, the region finds itself becoming increasingly interdependent with, and exposed to, global trends, whether in the international trading environment or in the changing context of East–West relations. Thus, in terms of the twin themes of this book – growth and interdependence – the balance of opportunity versus risk is by no means tipped unequivocally in favour of the former. How, then, should we weigh up the factors examined in the preceding chapters when considering the prospects for the region in the 1990s?

THE END OF HISTORY?

Communism emerged into world history as a frontal challenge to the core values of Western civilization and as such forced the Western world to mobilize all its military and economic resources to combat and contain its threat. In the event, thanks primarily to the massive power and wealth of the United States, the West has emerged as victor, although the military, political and socio-economic costs of the struggle were extremely high – not just for the United States and the Western allies, but also for Third World countries which were often sidetracked from their legitimate pursuit of growth.

Given that the Bush–Gorbachev summit in Malta in December 1989 declared the cold war at an end, does this spell the 'end of history', as Francis Fukuyama seems to suggest,[1] in the sense that there will no longer be a need for confrontation in the world, since everybody will now have to live by the norms and ideals of liberal democracy? Will this then lead to a grand revival of Western values as the dominant belief-system of the world? The vast land-mass of the northern hemisphere, from eastern Siberia to Western Europe to North America, seems to be turning into a citadel of Western democracy based on a potentially thriving market econ-omy.[2] Yet for many of the emerging democracies of Eastern Europe, de-Sovietization does not automatically lead to 'European-ization'. In trying to cope with the culture-shock of freedom while still in the midst of serious economic difficulties, these countries have begun to display a growing nationalism. The role of the West in preventing a repetition of history, a reversion to aggressive nationalism, is clearly going to be crucial.

In Pacific Asia, undoubtedly, nationalism has played a pivotal role in shaping political identities and national strategies in the post-colonial era, even though it is still possible to discern beneath the surface the continuing legacies of past 'ideologies', such as Confucianism, in the northeast Pacific Asian countries.[3] As the Cambodian–Vietnamese conflict has shown, to take just one example, traditional antagonisms may have been subdued, but they have not been eliminated by the development or imposition of either Western democratic pluralism or (originally European) social-democratic centralism. It is less easy, therefore, to see Fuku-yama's thesis being extended to Pacific Asia.

MAINTAINING THE STATUS QUO?

Despite the sudden collapse of communism in the East European states, their counterparts in Pacific Asia have managed to hold their ground, and even to maintain a semblance of an ideological divide between themselves and their former associates. And indeed differences do exist. Communism in Asia, as opposed to the West-ern variety, was seldom regarded as a challenge to the region's core value-system. For many in Pacific Asia, stability and growth has, in any case, been more valued than democracy and human rights. So communism was presented as one of the many formulas for modernization, although it was generally recognized as being more effective in destroying the *ancien régime* than in accelerating the process of economic development. Its demise in Eastern Europe, therefore, did not cause the same sense of elation and relief as in the West. As a result, in contrast with socialist Europe, which is in the process of major and largely irreversible change, socialist Pacific Asia seems to be more or less content with the status quo.

It was China's action in Tiananmen Square in June 1989 which, more than anything else, helped to determine this course for the Pacific Asian socialist states. In a sense, China and the Soviet Union had taken different paths to cope with essentially the same problem: whether, for the sake of national vitality, there should be a transition from one-party rule and planned development to pluralistic politics and market economy, and, if so, how it should be managed. The Soviet Union moved very quickly from political to economic change, which, as things turned out, has threatened the very foundation of the nation. China chose to start with economic reform, and, after wavering long over the extent of political change that it could allow, had to resort to the armed repression of demonstrators, at the risk of setting itself at odds with the outside world. Although the act of repression itself was deplorable, if China had given in at that juncture to the pressure of 'democratic' forces, it might have unleashed a tremendous confusion and chaos, even more difficult to contain than anything that the Soviet Union may have to face.

However, for all the power and control which China's communist party had thus managed to preserve, it is not very likely that the current state of affairs can be maintained indefinitely. The half-hearted implementation of the open-door policy since June 1989 seems to have aggravated the problems of the already stagnant economy; this will inevitably increase public dissatisfaction with the regime. The death of Deng Xiaoping, surely likely in the early 1990s, will lead to a renewed struggle for power within the leadership. The ongoing process of Hong Kong's return in 1997 may also pose a difficult challenge to the regime, to say nothing of the threat involved in the rapidly increasing economic and social links with Taiwan. China is slowly emerging from its pariah status, but the process of restoring commercial and diplomatic contacts with the West has taken far longer than the Chinese leaders anticipated. Although the community of fate with the Soviet Union still holds, China now has few ideological soul-mates left; economic imperatives will certainly make Vietnam and North Korea move further towards opening up during the next few years.

RETAINING THE US PRESENCE

Virtually all the countries in the region are continuing to formulate their policies on the assumption that the United States will maintain its presence in Pacific Asia – albeit in a slightly reduced form – in the post-cold-war era. Moreover, whereas in Europe the involvement of the United States is institutionalized in multiple layers of international forums and organizations, its presence in Pacific Asia is largely based on bilateral agreements, and therefore the impact of any change in US policy would be more direct and sharp.

Japan's peculiar dependence on the United States for its international position and role also has implications for the region. The US forces in Japan not only guarantee Japan's own security but also play an important role in regional politics by providing a credible deterrence to Japan's possible remilitarization. Past stability on the Korean peninsula has been largely due to the USA's presence there, so the nature of its future involvement will be important in determining any prospective moves towards unification on the part of the two Koreas. Likewise, the network of US bases in Japan, Okinawa and the Philippines has played an effective role in curbing Vietnamese and Chinese ambitions, as well as Soviet influences. Although ASEAN maintains a neutralist stance, it accepts the US presence in Pacific Asia as being both benign and desirable. In general, then, the countries of the region favour a continued American presence.

On the other hand, in the United States, domestic pressures for cutting back its military commitment abroad are bound to increase, if only for budgetary reasons. In addition, the surge of anti-Americanism in places like South Korea and the Philippines, and the unending trade conflicts with Japan (and now with the NIEs as well), might alienate official and public opinion in the United States *vis-à-vis* Pacific Asia. However, it would be premature and unwise for the United States to consider total withdrawal from Asia, given the fact that it is now the only functioning superpower in the world, and that Pacific Asia has long been its near-exclusive sphere of influence. Even though the forward deployment of US forces in the Philippines (which will end sooner rather than later) and other parts of the region will be phased down in the first half of the 1990s, the United States will undoubtedly find new formulas, such as burden-sharing, to maintain its influence but reduce its costs.

JAPAN'S POSITION AND ROLE

Japan, conversely, has an important role in determining the nature and scope of the US involvement in the region. The emerging framework of policy coordination and burden-sharing under the concept of 'global partnership' may be decisive in shaping the USA's future Asia policy. US–Japan cooperation will remain a key underpinning of the region's stability and prosperity. Some may fear a US–Japan condominium, but the region is likely to live with this as a lesser evil than Japan's going it alone, with all the unsettling implications that that has.

Despite the sometimes wishful thinking abroad, the powerful sun of Japan's economy is not yet ready to set. Japan's external surpluses will probably continue to shrink, but not as dramatically as they have done in 1988–9; Japan will begin to demonstrate that it has emerged stronger than ever from the economic restructuring wrought by the high yen. Commanding almost half of the region's GNP, its economic influence over Pacific Asia, through its immense trade, FDI, aid and technology transfer, is pervasive. From being solely an exporter of manufactured goods and an importer of raw materials, its steadily expanding capacity to absorb the region's own manufactures is providing a new factor in Pacific Asian industrialization and interdependence.

Nevertheless, post-war Japan has remained by and large detached from and hesitant in regional affairs, persistently avoiding a central role, under the convenient guise of an 'omnidirectional' foreign policy. As a result, its involvement in the region has not been properly evaluated or exploited for what it is: namely, the single most important input into the region's industrial growth. It is important that Japan's single-minded pursuit of its own development should change in the 1990s, when tremendous economic growth is likely to coincide with difficult political change. The other countries in the region must learn to accept its leadership in all kinds of economic skills, and Japan, for its part, must assume more responsibility for the region. This entails Japan facing its past squarely and reconciling itself to its history. Whether or not it can force itself to go through this painful but productive process will make a considerable difference to the region's, as well as Japan's, future.

REDUCTION OF REGIONAL TENSIONS

With the end of cold-war confrontation, the future shape of the Korean peninsula now lies essentially in the hands of the Koreans themselves, particularly of those in the North. Although it will take time for the North to move towards actual reunification, given the considerable uncertainties of its own regime as well as the unpredictability of its only ally and mentor, China, a gradual reduction in tension is not totally beyond the realms of possibility. However, reunification would lead to the emergence of a major economic and military power, with a combined population of 70 million, whose impact on Pacific Asia would be comparable with that of unified East and West Germany on Europe, and therefore will require a region-wide consensus on its ultimate shape, position and role. Yet even South Korea has not been able to build trust and credibility among its neighbours in the way that West Germany tried to do in Europe. The peculiar political underdevelopment of Northeast Asia provides some uncertainty for the 1990s.

Whereas the Korean peninsula has long been settled into a state that is really neither war nor peace, the Cambodian situation has once again returned to an active state of war. Although the Vietnamese troops have been withdrawn from Cambodia, and the external powers most interested, even China, are now concerned to bring about some solution, the four warring factions still refuse fully to accept and to implement a succession of peace plans that have been put forward. Even though growing popular distaste in the West for a return to power of the Khmer Rouge is bringing about a change in governmental (most notably US) approaches, the 'killing fields' are set to continue for some time.

By contrast, Vietnam, caught between a 'defecting' Soviet Union and a stagnating China, is likely to be more responsive to overtures from the fast-growing ASEAN countries, as well as to accept a market economy and a measure of pluralistic politics. No longer a divided country, its entry into 'free' Southeast Asia would not involve as many problems as in the case of Korea. Rather, it is likely to be welcomed as a source of stability as well as a new economic opportunity. The uniquely tolerant and pragmatic approach for which ASEAN is known will certainly facilitate Vietnam's participation in Southeast Asia. Even the possibility of some form of membership in ASEAN cannot be ruled out. With a commendable record of successful management of the region's stability and growth for more than two decades, ASEAN could certainly accommodate Vietnamese participation, and its own position and role would be strengthened in the process.

INTERDEPENDENCE AND REGIONAL CONSCIOUSNESS

Whereas the region is clearly increasing its internal economic interdependence, its interdependence with extra-regional partners is expanding even faster. In the second half of the 1980s, a great deal of the region's economy was incorporated into, or pulled along by, Japan's rapidly globalizing economy. Japan will, in part, replace the United States as an engine of growth for the region, but new markets in other parts of the globe will be sought as well. Extra-regional markets will indeed remain a lifeline for the NIEs, while ASEAN's exports, too, will reach the ends of the earth, riding on Western, Japanese and NIE manufacturing FDI. As the NIEs switch from being solely recipients of aid and FDI to being providers as well, they will tend to follow Japan in assuming a higher global economic profile, knocking on the door of the main international organizations such as the OECD. Certainly, growing protectionism in Western markets, the instability of oil prices, the effective crowding out of Western, including even Japanese, industrial capital by the need for East European development, and the continual challenge of technological upgrading will be outstanding concerns for the 1990s. Nevertheless, World Bank estimates for the decade of the 1990s still put Pacific Asia at the top of the regional growth table, with an average of 6.6 per cent per annum, more than double the projected growth figure for the industrialized world.[4]

Efforts towards regional economic cooperation as seen in such fora as PECC and APEC will continue, although full-scale economic integration is unlikely, at least for the time being. Apart from the fact that the region's economies are more in competition with one another than complementary, there is little inclination to accept arrangements that entail subordinating sovereign rights. Moreover, ASEAN's reluctance to accept any forum that might dilute its influence will continue to play an important restraining role. Being the only functioning cooperative organization in the region, its bargaining position is unusually strong; even Japan tends to defer to it. ASEAN will act as the anchor of Pacific Asia, but neither it nor, indeed, APEC has the potential to be on a par with either the EC or the North American trading blocs. There may, indeed, be cross-cutting tendencies deriving from small economic sub-groups, such as the 'growth triangle' concept involving Singapore with parts of neighbouring Malaysia and Indonesia, and Thailand's 'golden peninsula' ambitions, or from more nebulous networking, such as the 'greater China' entrepreneurial links.

Nevertheless, the growth in Pacific Asian regional consciousness, partly in response to regionalist moves elsewhere in the global community, will continue, though it will be a slow process. In Europe, the disintegration of the socialist East has, somewhat surprisingly, given added impetus to the already fast-moving process of West European integration. In Pacific Asia there is neither the internal political will nor the external catalyst to spur economic, let alone political, integration beyond a cautious forward pace. Indeed, the Pacific Asian economy aspires to a global rather than a regional role, partly because its dynamism seems at times too strong to be confined within the region, and partly because extra-regional countries wish to benefit from Asian competitive manufacturing systems (for example, Britain in 1989 became a net exporter of televisions, thanks to Japanese FDI).

PACIFIC ASIAN SOCIETY

Even though the elites, let alone the broad masses, of the region are finding it difficult to think 'Pacific Asian', perhaps it is possible to discern some commonalities emerging across the region's societies. The current realities of the world dictate that non-Western developing nations accept a measure of westernization in their modernization efforts, at the inevitable risk of a certain conflict with their traditional cultures. Each and every nation in the region has been obliged, though in different degrees, to grapple with this problem according to its individual historical and cultural environment, and the process has invariably left its scars. But the fact that the region has constantly had to face these inner strains may have helped it to steer away from complacency and stagnation, and may have kept it receptive to new ideas. However, unless and until it manages to arrive at a creative fusion of its many cultures, and to generate a value-system of its own, it will find it difficult to claim its rightful place in the world.

The region's traumatic post-war experiences, whether the struggles for independence or democratization, occupation by the United States, or outright communist revolution, had the combined effect of destroying the power of yesterday's privileged classes, enabling most countries to start with a clean slate and to experiment with a variety of formulas, whether 'military-led growth' or 'capitalistic socialism'. Admittedly, there are remaining bastions of oligarchical power in the Philippines or the hereditary authority of sultans in Malaysia and Brunei, and the problem of an unequal distribution of income still remains serious in several countries, yet a new and prosperous middle-class is springing up across the region. Moreover, these newly rich show little sign so far of becoming the latter-day oligarchy, and it is to be hoped that further progress in non-elitist growth, and diffusion of the benefits of that growth, will be made.

One of the forces behind Pacific Asia's current growth thrust seems to be its unabashed appetite for consumption. People do not shy away from the attractions of wealth, and are gladly enthralled by the glitter of the latest gadgets and gewgaws. A continuous flow of new products keeps whetting consumer appetites, thereby further stimulating the regional economy. A staggering number of tourists swarm over the length and breadth of the region on a perpetual shopping spree, expanding the region's economic base. Many of the region's economies were aided in their earlier development by the high savings rates achieved; this is likely to change as people switch to consumerism. Consumerism, however, when carried to excess, can lead to domestic tensions between the 'haves' and 'have-nots'; South Korea is not alone in wanting to discourage conspicuous over-consumption (especially of imported luxury goods). Moreover, the attractions of a better standard of living are leading to flows of people not only from rural to urban areas within countries, but also from poor countries to richer ones.

As a result, new patterns of affluence are being created across the region. Demographic changes play a part, too, as the trend towards smaller families and more new households begins to make itself felt. Consumer demand and tourism will undoubtedly continue to grow, but, since the taste for international travel and Western goods is also likely to increase, such influences will expand global, rather than solely regional, ties and cut across the emergence of any real Pacific Asian society.[5]

PACIFIC CENTURY?

The notion of a Pacific Century, in which the Pacific Asian region would play the lead, has tended to evaporate since the end of the cold war and the return of Europe to centre-stage. The coincidence of change in global politico-strategic relations with the EC's endeavour for single-market integration, combined with the challenge of the new East European economies, has revitalized Europe, and, by extension, the United States. The psychological boost has been such that some Europeans – German Chancellor Helmut Kohl for one – even see the 1990s as the 'decade of Europe'. Although it is still possible that the Western economy could get mired either in possible chaos and confusion in Eastern Europe (including the Soviet Union) or in prolonged instability in the Middle East, the scenario of 'the decline of the West' has been rendered unlikely. Moreover, the sea-change in Europe in 1989–90 has brought into sharper focus a set of political difficulties in the Pacific Asian region which could very well retard the seemingly relentless momentum of its growth, undermining the idea of the Pacific Century, at least in the simplistic sense of replacing previous – Western – centuries.

What is clear, however, is that the Pacific Asian region's weight and involvement in global affairs will continue to increase as the next century approaches. Given that, on balance, the economic growth prognosis for the region is favourable, international economic organizations, such as the World Bank, the IMF and the OECD, will have to adjust not merely to the enhanced standing of Japan but also to the arrival of the NIEs to economic maturity. Moreover, Pacific Asia's voice in global security matters can no longer be ignored; as the European scene is transformed, and NATO and the Warsaw Pact lose their original justifications, so superpower attention will shift to promoting reconciliation in the Pacific Asian region. As regards the newer items on the international agenda – drugs, terrorism, migration and the environment – as well as the lingering problems of Third World, especially African, development, Pacific Asian countries will want, and will be expected, to play a more active role.

The question remains, nevertheless, whether the world will continue to be governed essentially by Western values and systems in the coming century, or whether another set of values will emerge to share the position of leadership. The triumph of the Western system dates from its success in the nineteenth-century industrial revolution, which enabled the West to monopolize the instruments of control, such as military strength and industrial power. In addition, the form of pluralistic democracy developed by the British, with later versions grafted on by the Americans, was accepted broadly as the most viable formula of management for modern states. It was further enhanced and improved by competition and rivalry among the Europeans, as well as a productive interaction across the Atlantic. Its latest victory over communism is the result not only of the West's military power but also of the effectiveness of its economic management, combined with a broad acceptance by the non-Western world of democratic values.

Fragmented historically and geographically, non-Western values and traditions were not able to take a full part in shaping the modern global civilization, while centuries of colonial domination sapped the morale, confidence and vitality of much of the non-Western world. However, there are Asian values and social norms that are relevant in the current world. Pacific Asia's model for national economic growth, for example, could be a valuable source of assistance to Third World development, which will perhaps become the main item on the agenda of the post-cold-war period. Even Eastern Europe may benefit from the Pacific model. Already many of the Asian attitudes and norms are being integrated into the Western system by means of Pacific Asia's vigorous FDI in manufacturing in the United States and Europe. If, as seems likely, Pacific Asia keeps growing in the 1990s, this trend will accelerate. Even though the Pacific Century itself may never materialize, the region will surely take a more prominent place in the world of the twenty-first century.

Notes

CHAPTER 1

THE REGION'S ECONOMY: PATTERNS OF PROSPERITY

An earlier version of much of this chapter appeared in article form as Kate Grosser and Brian Bridges, 'Economic Interdependence in East Asia: the Global Context', *The Pacific Review*, Vol. 3, No. 1 (1990).

1 Ronald Dore, *Flexible Rigidities* (London: Athlone, 1986), pp. 12–58.
2 Keizai Koho Center, *Japan 1990* (Tokyo, 1990).
3 *Japan* (London: Japan Information Centre), 15 September 1988.
4 See Helen Hughes (ed.), *Achieving Industrialization in East Asia* (Cambridge: Cambridge University Press, 1988).
5 According to one estimate, Japanese FDI contributed 7% of the growth in nominal GDP in Indonesia during 1965–85. David Robins, 'Japan: a New Role in the Pacific?' UBS/Philips and Drew, 9 November 1987.
6 'Japan in the Nineties' (Amsterdam: NRI for Nomura Capital Management, December 1989).
7 The data on which the discussion is based is presented in more detail in Kate Grosser and Brian Bridges, 'Economic Interdependence in East Asia', *The Pacific Review*, Vol. 3, No. 1 (1990), pp. 9–11.
8 *Far Eastern Economic Review*, 2 February 1989; *BBC Summary of World Broadcasts*, FE/W0103, 15 November 1989.
9 For a discussion of these issues, see Peter Buckley and Hafiz Mirza, 'The Strategy of Pacific Asian Multinationals', *The Pacific Review*, Vol. 1, No. 1 (1988), pp. 50–62.
10 The FDI pattern is similar for the EC during the 1980s, for the increases in British, French and German FDI have gone predominantly to the United States. See DeAnne Julius and Stephen Thomsen, *Foreign Direct Investment among the G-5*, RIIA Discussion Paper No. 8 (London: Royal Institute of International Affairs, 1988), pp. 6–7.

11 Dennis Yasumoto, 'Nihon Gaiko to ODA Seisaku', *Kokusai Mondai*, March 1989, pp. 37–54.
12 *Japan Economic Journal*, 15 July 1989.
13 DeAnne Julius and Stephen Thomsen, *Inward Investment and Foreign-owned Firms in the G-5*, RIIA Discussion Paper No. 12 (London: Royal Institute of International Affairs, 1989), pp. 31–2.
14 Hugh Patrick, 'The Beginning of the American Economic Stake in the Pacific Basin', background paper for Joint Economic Committee of US Congress Symposium on US–Pacific Rim Relations (Washington DC: USGPO, 1987), p. 73.
15 Brian Bridges, 'Deepening the EC–Korean Relationship', *Korea and World Affairs*, Spring 1990, pp. 67–82.

CHAPTER 2

THE SECURITY CONTEXT: REGION IN FLUX

1 See the remarks of Brigadier-General George Yeo, Singapore's Minister of State for Foreign Affairs, in *World Link*, No. 7/8 (July/August 1990), p. 34.
2 Edwin Simmons, 'Korea to Kampuchea: the Changing Nature of Warfare in East Asia 1950–86, Part I', in *East Asia, the West and International Security: Prospects for Peace*, Adelphi Papers No. 216 (London: International Institute for Strategic Studies, 1987), p. 71.
3 For the texts of the Vladivostok and Krasnoyarsk speeches, see *Soviet News*, 30 July 1986 and 21 September 1988.
4 US Department of Defense, *A Strategic Framework for the Asian Pacific Rim: Looking Toward the 21st Century*, April 1990, p. 8.
5 *A Strategic Framework*, pp. 9–44 ff.
6 Ibid.
7 Ibid.
8 John M. Collins, *US–Soviet Military Balance 1980–1985* (Washington DC: Pergamon/Brassey's, 1985), p. 142.
9 Zakaria Haji Ahmad, 'Images of American Power: Perspectives from Southeast Asia', *Asian Defence Journal*, May 1991.
10 Samuel Huntington, 'The United States: Decline or Renewal?', in Adelphi Paper No. 235 (London: International Institute for Strategic Studies, 1989), pp.63–80. The foremost book that argues the inevitability of US decline is of course Paul Kennedy's *The Rise and Fall of the Great Powers* (New York: Random House, 1987). For a journalistic rejection of US decline, see Karen Elliott House, 'Is US Declining as World Power? Only Americans Seem to Think So,' *Asian Wall Street Journal*, 24 January 1989, p.20.
11 The notion that the US is the 'world's number one debtor nation' has been disputed by Charles Wolf and Sarah Hooker in their 'Who Owes Whom and How Much?', *Asian Wall Street Journal*, 11 January 1988.

12 Richard Nixon, 'On World Leadership's Indispensable Ingredient', *Life*, October 1987, pp. 30–1.
13 Donald Zagoria, 'Soviet Policy in East Asia: A New Beginning?', *Foreign Affairs*, Vol. 68, No. 1 (1989), pp. 120–38.
14 For a view of the Chinese position, see Chen Qingliang, 'Kampuchea: the Political Settlement Tangle' (Beijing: China Institute of Contemporary International Relations, October 1988), mimeograph. See also Gerald Segal, *The Soviet Union and the Pacific* (London: Unwin Hyman/Royal Institute of International Affairs, 1990), pp. 113–15.
15 Kenneth Hunt, 'Japan's Security Policy', in *Survival*, May/June 1989, p. 201.
16 *Straits Times*, 9 May 1990; *Far Eastern Economic Review*, 24 May 1990.
17 *Far Eastern Economic Review*, 13 September 1990; William Turley, 'The Khmer War: Cambodia after Paris', *Survival*, September/October 1990, pp. 437–53.
18 Brian Bridges, *Korea and the West*, Chatham House Paper No. 33 (London: Routledge/Royal Institute of International Affairs, 1986), pp. 43–8.
19 Dan Sanford, *South Korea and the Socialist Countries* (London: Macmillan, 1990).
20 *Japan Economic Journal*, 6 and 13 October 1990.
21 Donald Wetherbee, 'The South China Sea: from Zone of Conflict to Zone of Peace', in Lawrence Grinter and Young Whan Kihl (eds.), *East Asian Conflict Zones* (London: Macmillan, 1987), pp. 123–48; *Far Eastern Economic Review*, 31 March 1988.
22 Mark Valencia, 'The Spratly Islands: Dangerous Ground in the South China Sea', *Pacific Review*, Vol. 1, No. 4 (1988), pp. 438–43.
23 Wolfram Wallraf, 'Common Security in the Pacific: Another European View', *Pacific Review*, Vol. 2, No. 3 (1989), pp. 226–35. See also Gerald Segal, *Rethinking the Pacific* (Oxford: Oxford University Press, 1990), pp. 261–79.
24 Young-Koo Cha, 'Arms Talks on the Korean Peninsula: A Korean Perspective', *Korean Journal of International Studies*, Summer 1990, pp. 234–8.
25 *Nikon Keizai Shimbun*, 25 July and 6 September 1990.
26 US Department of Defense, *A Strategic Framework*, pp. 4–5. For a discussion of these issues, see Roger A. Brooks (ed.), *US Policy in Asia: The Challenges for 1990*, Heritage Lectures 233 (Washington DC: Heritage Foundation, 1990).
27 Brigadier General Lee Hsien Loong, 'The FPDA and Regional Stability', opening speech for the air defence seminar of the Five-Power Defence Agreements, 29 November 1989. This speech is reproduced in *Asian Defence Journal*, February 1990, pp. 28–31.

CHAPTER 3

THE DEVELOPMENTAL STATE: A TENTATIVE FRAMEWORK

1 *The Emerging Japanese Super-state* (Englewood Cliffs, NJ: Prentice-Hall, 1970).
2 *Japan as Number One* (New York: Harper and Row, 1979).
3 *Asia–Pacific Report, Trends, Issues, Challenges: 1978–88* (Honolulu: East–West Center, 1987), p. 2.
4 J. Morley and S. Ichimura, 'The Anomalies of the Asia–Pacific Experience', in J. Morley (ed.), *Economic Growth and Political Change in Pacific Asia* (forthcoming).
5 *Asia–Pacific Report*, p. 5.
6 Lucian W. Pye, *Asian Power and Politics, the Cultural Dimension of Authority* (Cambridge, MA: The Belknap Press of Harvard University Press, 1985), p. 2. Emphasis added.
7 Roy Hofheinz Jr. and Kent E. Calder, *The East/Asia Edge* (New York: Basic Books, 1982).
8 Myron Weiner, 'Introduction', in Myron Weiner and Samuel P. Huntington (eds.), *Understanding Political Development* (Boston: Little Brown, 1987), p. xx.
9 For an analysis of the nature of authoritarian rule in the region, see Jean-Pierre Lehmann, 'Dictatorship and Development in Pacific Asia: Wider Implications', *International Affairs*, Vol. 61, No. 4 (Autumn 1985), pp. 591–606.
10 On this concept, see Hyug Beg Im, 'The Rise of Bureaucratic Authoritarianism in South Korea', *World Politics*, Vol. 39 (January 1987).
11 *Japan as Number One*, pp. 53–96.
12 Chalmers Johnson, *MITI and the Japanese Miracle* (Stanford: Stanford University Press, 1982).
13 Peter Evans, 'Foreign Capital and the Third World State', in Weiner and Huntington, *Understanding Political Development*, pp. 310–52.
14 Takashi Inoguchi, 'Four Japanese Scenarios for the Future', *International Affairs*, Vol. 65, No. 1 (Winter, 1988/89), pp. 15–28.
15 See In-Joung Whang, *Management of Rural Change in Korea: The Saemaul Undong* (Seoul: Seoul National University Press, 1981).
16 Robert Scalapino, 'Political Trends in Asia and Their Implications for the Region', in Robert Scalapino, *et al.* (eds.), *Asia and the Major Powers* Institute of East Asian Studies Research Papers and Policy Studies No. 28 (Berkeley: University of California Press, 1988), pp. 365–84.
17 Ibid.
18 See also the discussion in John Girling, 'Development and Democracy in Southeast Asia', *The Pacific Review*, Vol. 1, No. 4 (1988), pp. 332–40.

CHAPTER 4

THE NEWLY INDUSTRIALIZING ECONOMIES

1 For excellent studies of the economic development of the NIEs, see Louis Turner and Neil McMullen, *The Newly Industrializing Countries: Trade and Adjustment* (London: Allen & Unwin/Royal Institute of International Affairs, 1982), and Helen Hughes (ed.), *Achieving Industrialization in East Asia* (Cambridge: Cambridge University Press, 1988).

2 See Hong Nack Kim, 'The 1988 Parliamentary Election in South Korea', *Asian Survey*, May 1989, pp. 480–95.

3 Hakjoon Kim, 'New Political Development with a Vision for the 1990s and Beyond', *Korea and World Affairs*, Spring 1990, pp. 34–53.

4 An example of the debate over liberalization can be found in the paper by Soo-gil Young and Korean commentators' remarks in Thomas Bayard and Soo-gil Young (eds.), *Economic Relations between the United States and Korea: Conflict or Cooperation?* (Washington, DC: Institute of International Economics, 1989), pp. 119–68.

5 Kim Hwang-joe, 'Labour Movement in Korea: Present Status and Perspectives', in Dalchoong Kim and Graham Healey (eds.), *Korea and the United Kingdom* (Institute of East and West Studies, Yonsei, Seoul, 1990), pp. 153–81.

6 See contributions by Michael Smith and Jeffrey Schott to Bayard and Young, *Economic Relations*, pp. 77–117.

7 *Korea Newsreview*, 24 February 1990.

8 Hee Mock Noh, 'The Development of Korean Trade and Investment in the PRC', *Korea and World Affairs*, Fall 1989, pp. 421–39.

9 *Korea Times*, 23 and 24 March 1990; *International Herald Tribune*, 7 and 8 June 1990.

10 *Korea Newsreview*, 27 February 1988.

11 Walter Arnold, 'Science and Technology Development in Taiwan and South Korea', *Asian Survey*, April 1988, pp. 437–50.

12 *Far Eastern Economic Review*, 6 July 1989.

13 Hung-mo Tien, 'The Transformation of an Authoritarian Party-State; Taiwan's Developmental Experience', *Issues and Studies*, July 1989, p. 118.

14 *Far Eastern Economic Review*, 29 March 1990.

15 Dame Lydia Dunn, speaking in London in February 1990, quoted estimates of manufacturing jobs for 2 million Chinese in the Pearl River Delta in some 18,000 factories processing goods for Hong Kong companies; *Dateline Hong Kong*, No. 3, 1990.

16 Dick Wilson, *Hong Kong's Future: Realistic Grounds for Optimism?* RIIA Discussion Paper No. 29 (London: Royal Institute of International Affairs, 1990).

17 Joseph Y. S. Cheng, 'The Democracy Movement in Hong Kong', *International Affairs*, Summer 1989, pp. 443–62.

18 *The Independent*, 13 February 1990.

19 Ibid., 5 April 1990. Deng Xiaoping described the Basic Law as 'a masterpiece of creativity'; *The Observer*, 18 February 1990.

20 *The Guardian*, 5 April 1990.
21 Stuart Drummond, 'Malaysia and Singapore: Strains and Stresses at Both Ends of the Causeway', *The World Today*, April 1989, pp. 69–70.
22 *Far Eastern Economic Review*, 19 May 1988.

CHAPTER 5

SOUTHEAST ASIA: UNITY WITHIN DIVERSITY

1 On dynamism, see Takashi Inoguchi, 'Shaping and Sharing Pacific Dynamism', *The Annals of the American Academy of Political and Social Science*, September 1989. According to Inoguchi, dynamism has both 'positive' and 'negative' aspects.
2 As summarized by Catherine Gwin, 'Introduction', in Guy Pauker, Frank Golay and Cynthia Enloe, *Diversity and Development in Southeast Asia: The Coming Decade* (New York: McGraw-Hill for the Council on Foreign Relations, 1977), p. 3.
3 Robert Scalapino, 'An External Perspective on Southeast Asian Politics', in Karl D. Jackson *et al.* (eds.), *ASEAN in Regional and Global Context* (Berkeley: University of California Institute of East Asian Studies Research Papers and Policy Studies, 1986), p. 17.
4 See Harold Crouch, 'Economic Growth and Democratization in Southeast Asia', in James Morley (ed.), *Economic Growth and Political Change in Pacific Asia* (forthcoming).
5 See the perceptive observations of Kernial Sandhu in his 'Southeast Asia: Politics in Context', in Jackson, *ASEAN*, pp. 26–9.
6 Sukhumbhand Paribatra, 'The Challenge of Coexistence: ASEAN's Relations with Vietnam in the 1990s' in *Contemporary Southeast Asia*, Vol. 9, No. 2 (1987), p. 140.
7 *ASEAN: the Way Forward*, Report of the Group of Fourteen on ASEAN Economic Cooperation and Integration (Kuala Lumpur: ISIS, for the ASEAN Chambers of Commerce and Industry, 1987), p. 61. The G-14 is a group composed of the representatives of the ASEAN Chambers of Commerce and Industry, and therefore essentially a private-sector initiative.
8 See, e.g., Zakaria Haji Ahmad (ed.), *Japan–United States Relations and the Asia-Pacific* (Kuala Lumpur: Malaysian International Relations Forum, 1987).
9 Takashi Inoguchi, 'Four Japanese Scenarios for the Future', *International Affairs*, Vol. 65, No. 1 (1988/89), pp. 15–28.
10 See Zakaria Haji Ahmad (ed.), *The Five-Power Defence Arrangements and Southeast Asian Security* (forthcoming).
11 Linda Martin (ed.), *The ASEAN Success Story* (Honolulu: University of Hawaii Press, 1986).
12 Zakaria Haji Ahmad, 'Introduction', in 'ASEAN in the 1990s', *Contemporary Southeast Asia*, September 1987, p. 85.
13 Donald E. Weatherbee, 'ASEAN Security Issues in the 1990s: a World Turned Upside Down', paper read at the Defence Services Asia 1990

Conference 'Defence for Development in Pacific-Asia', 21–22 March 1990.

14 On an overview analysis of ASEAN economic cooperation, see Hans Christoph Rieger, 'Regional Economic Cooperation in the Asia–Pacific Region', in *Asia–Pacific Economic Literature*, Vol. 3, No. 2 (1989), pp. 5–33.

15 Third ASEAN Round Table, *ASEAN Cooperation in a Changing International Environment*, a summary record (Singapore: Institute of Southeast Asian Studies, 16–17 January 1989), p. 1.

16 Fourth ASEAN Round Table, *ASEAN Cooperation: Agenda for the 1990s* (Singapore: Institute of Southeast Asian Studies, 29–30 March 1990).

17 See *ASEAN-US Initiative, Joint Final Report* (Honolulu: East–West Center, and Singapore: Institute of Southeast Asian Studies, 1989).

18 See Zakaria Haji Ahmad, 'ASEAN and Asia-Pacific Cooperation: the Political Dimension', paper read at the Thammasat University Conference 'Cooperation in Asia–Pacific: the Role of Japan, USA, China, NICs and ASEAN', Bangkok, 2–3 March 1990.

19 See Zakaria Haji Ahmad, 'The World of ASEAN Decision-Makers: a Study of Elite Bureaucratic Perceptions in Malaysia, the Philippines and Singapore', *Contemporary Southeast Asia*, Vol. 8, No. 3 (1986).

CHAPTER 6

CHINA AND THE SOCIALIST STATES

1 Economic Section, American Embassy, *Foreign Economic Trends* (Beijing: July 1985).

2 Toshio Watanabe, 'Chugoku keizai no "zasetsu" to "kibo"', *Voice*, July 1989, pp. 122–40.

3 Robert Field, 'Changes in Chinese Industry since 1978', *China Quarterly*, December 1984, pp. 742–61; *Far Eastern Economic Review*, 8 September 1988.

4 David S. G. Goodman, Martin Lockett and Gerald Segal, *The China Challenge* (London: Routledge/Royal Institute of International Affairs, 1986), p. 18. See also Toshio Watanabe (as in n. 2), pp. 122–40.

5 Deng Xiaoping, conversation in Beijing, with visiting members of the Trilateral Commission, May 1980.

6 Quoted by Tony Saich, 'The Reform Process in the People's Republic of China', *Journal of Communist Studies*, March 1988, p. 13.

7 Lucian Pye, *Asian Power and Politics* (Cambridge, MA: The Belknap Press of Harvard University Press, 1985), p. 189.

8 Decentralization and regionalization are explored in detail in David S. G. Goodman (ed.), *China's Regional Development* (London: Routledge/Royal Institute of International Affairs, 1989).

9 Pye, *Asian Power and Politics*, p. 184.

10 BBC, *Summary of World Broadcasts*, FE 0459, 17 May 1989.

11 Nakajima Mineo, *Chugoku-no Higeki* (Tokyo: Kodansha, 1989), pp. 77–86.

12 *South China Morning Post*, 3 January 1991.
13 *Asian Wall Street Journal*, Tokyo, 31 December 1990.
14 Mori Kazuko, 'Teimeisuru chugokuseiji', *Kokusai Mondai*, No. 370, January 1991.
15 *Yomiuri Shimbun*, 17 March 1990; quoted in Mori Kazuko, 'Teimeisuru chugokuseiji', loc. cit.
16 Takagi Seiichiro, 'Resentaisei-no Hokai-to Chugoku-no Taigaikankei', *Kokusai Mondai*, No. 370, January 1991.
17 *The Economist*, 2–8 February 1991, p. 25.
118 See James Cotton, 'The Prospects of the North Korean Political Succession', *Korea and World Affairs*, Winter 1987, pp. 745–68.
19 See Brian Bridges, 'Awkward Ally: The Soviet View of North Korea', *Journal of Communist Studies*, March 1987, pp. 108–11.
20 JETRO, *Kitachosen no keizai to boeki no tenbo*, June 1988, August 1989 and October 1990.
21 *Asian Wall Street Journal*, 11 September 1989; *The Banker*, April 1990.
22 *Nation* (Bangkok), 9 September 1989.

CHAPTER 7

JAPAN AS FACILITATOR

1 See Marius Jensen (ed.), *Cambridge History of Japan*, Vol. 5, Nineteenth Century (Cambridge: Cambridge University Press, 1989), especially Chapters 5, 7, 11 and 12.
2 See Ramon Myers and Mark Peattie, *The Japanese Colonial Empire, 1895–1945* (Princeton: Princeton University Press, 1984).
3 See, e.g., Shibusawa Masahide, *Japan and the Asian Pacific Region* (London: Croom Helm/Royal Institute of International Affairs, 1984).
4 See I. M. Destler and Sato Hideo, *Coping with US–Japanese Economic Conflicts* (Lexington: Lexington Books, 1982).
5 J. A. A. Stockwin, *Japan: Divided Politics in a Growth Economy* (London: Weidenfeld & Nicolson, 1982), pp. 112–35.
6 For a detailed discussion, see Karel van Wolferen, *The Enigma of Japanese Power* (London: Macmillan, 1989), Chapter 5, 'The Administrators', pp. 109–58.
7 *New York Times*, 20 March 1990.
8 *Asian Wall Street Journal*, 25 May 1990.
9 Richard Mathews, ' "Kokusaika" tojokoku Nihon wa doko e yuku?', *Chuo Koron*, March 1990.
10 *Yomiuri Shimbun*, 6 January 1990.
11 Mathews (as in n. 9), p. 7. See also the discussion in Shiro Saito, *Japan at the Summit* (London: Routledge/Royal Institute of International Affairs, 1990), especially Chapter 1.
12 The concepts of 'challenger', etc., are taken from Takashi Inoguchi's introductory chapter to Takashi Inoguchi and Daniel Okimoto (eds.), *The Political Economy of Japan*, Vol. 2 (Stanford: Stanford University Press, 1988).

13 Dennis Yasutomo, 'Nihon gaiko to ODA seisaku', *Kokusai Mondai*, March 1989, pp. 37–54.
14 *Asian Wall Street Journal*, 5 January 1990.

CHAPTER 8

PACIFIC ASIA IN THE 1990s

1 For the full text of Fukuyama's article, see *The National Interest*, Summer 1989; for excerpts, see *The Independent*, 20 and 21 September 1989.
2 This idea has led to some visionary statements, such as that by Gianni de Michelis, the Italian Foreign Minister, in June 1990 about the reorganization of the space which 'extends from San Francisco to Vladivostok'. *Agence Europe*, 4 July 1990.
3 On the role of 'ideologies', see Gerald Segal, *Rethinking the Pacific* (Oxford: Oxford University Press, 1990), pp. 111–25.
4 World Bank, *World Development Report 1990* (Oxford, 1990), p. 16.
5 See, for example, Segal, *Rethinking the Pacific*, pp. 148–52, 179–82.

Index